A Nature and Hiking Guide to Cape Breton's Cabot Trail

A Nature and Hiking Guide to Cape Breton's Cabot Trail

David Lawley

NIMBUS
PUBLISHING

97 98 99   6 5 4 3 2

Nimbus Publishing Limited
PO Box 9301, Station A
Halifax, NS, B3K 5N5
(902) 455-4286

Design and Production: Bras d'Or Graphic Marketing Services
Woodcuts: Burland Murphy
Landscapes: Virginia McCoy
Woodpeckers: Barry Fraser
Assorted line drawings: Canadian Parks Service

Printed and bound in Canada

Canadian Cataloguing in Publication Data
Lawley, David.

A nature and hiking guide to Cape Breton's Cabot Trail
Includes bibliographical references.
ISBN 1-55109-105-4

1. Trails – Nova Scotia – Cape Breton Island – Guidebooks.
2. Hiking – Nova Scotia – Cape Breton Island – Guidebooks.
3. Cabot Trail (N.S.) – Guidebooks. 4. Cape Breton Island (N.S.) –
Guidebooks. I. Title.

GV199.44.C32N64 1994   917.16'9044   C94-950177-8

To Elaine,
the naturalist who opened the door,
allowing nature to seep, ever so slowly,
into my perception.

ACKNOWLEDGMENTS

Many thanks to the people and organizations who made this book possible. Thanks to ACOA and Les Amis du Plein Air for the financial help. A very special thank you to Nora Macnee and Jim Dale for their many hours smoothing out the rough edges, and for their endless support. Thanks to all the naturalists who walked the Trail before me, and recorded their experiences so I and others could benefit. Thank you to the staff of Cape Breton Highlands National Park, the Nova Scotia Museum and Nova Scotia Parks and Recreation Division for their good humour and team spirit which leaked into this book. And last but not least, thanks to William Armstrong, Derek Davis, Maureen Carroll, Barrie Fraser, Burland Murphy, Bill Fraser, Phil and Cathy Guest, Ken Lywood, Dave MacCorquodale, Jim Morrow, Jeff Pike, Ivo Potach, Pixie Williams and Margrit Gahlinger for their help in bringing this dream into reality.

CONTENTS

PART ONE

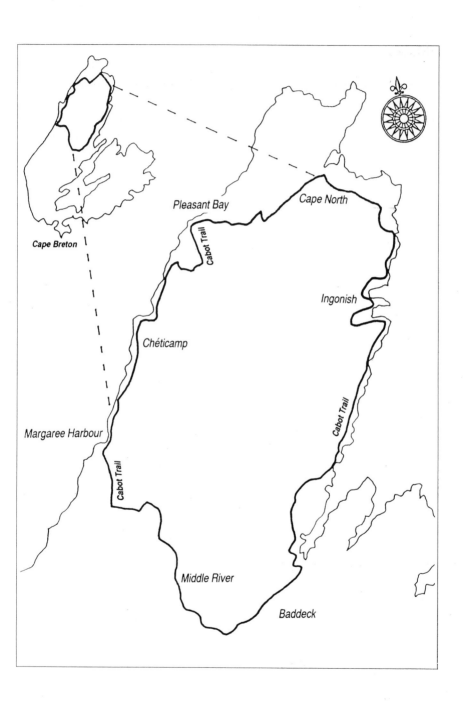

PREFACE

It is thought that three years after Christopher Columbus sailed to the Americas John Cabot sailed into Aspy Bay, Cape Breton. This is how the picturesque Cabot Trail that winds its way around northern Cape Breton received its name. The construction of this famous 289 kilometre road took place in the 1930s.

The information about the plants and animals found along the Cabot Trail has been accumulating since before the Trail itself was completed. The book attempts to gather together and update some of the knowledge we have about the natural history of the Trail. In doing so the book tries to present this knowledge to you, the ardent naturalist and visiting public alike, in an interesting and easy to read manner.

I hope this book will enrich your vacation and enliven your natural dreams.

David Lawley
Grand Étang, NS

INTRODUCTION

The Cabot Trail is a wonderfully scenic road that winds through the valleys and highlands of northern Cape Breton Island. The natural history of the Cabot Trail is the story of nature, of the animals and plants that live here. This book is written for you, the naturalist. It shows you where to find the trails, the animals, plants, and rocks - in short, all the natural beauty as you travel this famous road. We are going to drive the Cabot Trail together. We'll stop and explore every hiking trail along the way, meet some of the local people, and at times venture off the Trail to discover other treasures. There are over 10,000 different types of plants and animals in northern Cape Breton. We will discover many of these sometimes strange and always beautiful forms of life. But before we go, we have to take a small trip back through time, for a brief description of the history of the natural world which will help us appreciate our discoveries.

We, the Earth, along with our sun, have been orbiting the Milky Way galaxy since the beginning of our time, 4.6 billion years ago. We have circled the galaxy 21 times, with each orbit lasting 220 million years. Most of the rocks in Cape Breton were formed during the last four trips around the galaxy. As the ancient pre-Atlantic Ocean closed, all of the continents came together. In the process, three chips of land off the coasts of what are now Africa, South America and North America were squeezed between the continents. These formed the land mass which today is the island of Cape Breton. Geologists later named these chips the Aspy, the Bras d'Or and the Mira Terranes. When they collided, high mountains were formed and at the same time, plants and animals began to move out of the sea and on to the land.

Over time these high mountains of Cape Breton were eroded by wind and rain. Boulders and sand washed off the mountains and onto the lowlands. Some of these mountains were volcanoes spewing ash onto the land. Soon all that remained were lowlands, with limestone and gypsum in shallow seas. Swamps that created all the coal in Cape Breton were created next. The trees were actually 120 foot tall ferns and dragonflies were the size of sea gulls.

Then, 220 million years ago, we began our current trip around the galaxy. This orbit started during a fierce desert storm, with high winds and blowing sand. Most of the events of Cape Breton's geological past took place while it was still in the equatorial region. Then, new continents started to separate, creating the Atlantic Ocean. The island of Cape Breton, along with North America, moved to the northern hemisphere for the first time. Dinosaurs flourished in the Maritimes of Atlantic Canada. All of the land remained close to sea level until 65 million years ago, when the highlands of Cape Breton were roused out of their slumber and uplifted to about today's height of 500 meters. Glaciers followed, scouring the island, destroying the plants and causing the animals to flee. The ice sheet washed out the ancient riverways, pushing and depositing rubble and rock debris around the island. Finally, twelve thousand years ago, the weather started to resemble today's, and the old forest with its many creatures returned to Cape Breton.

As we go around the Cabot Trail in this book we'll look at the animals and plants of today. Each stop offers you a chance to peer into the great beauty of Cape Breton. There are checklists in the back of the book which include all of the plants, birds, mammals, amphibians and reptiles found in northern Cape Breton. I hope you enjoy the trip. So let's get started. We'll begin on the western side of Cape Breton where the coastal section of the Ceilidh Trail connects to the Cabot Trail at Margaree Harbour and we will travel the Cabot Trail clockwise. Many believe this is the preferred direction when driving because the vistas are more spectacular. See what you think. Bon voyage!

Cabot Trail - Cap Rouge Summit

The Cabot Trail

From Belle Côte to Chéticamp you can see the highlands looming off in the distance and a low flat plain that was once covered with a forest of mature sugar maple, ash, oak, and white pine. The English and French logged much of this area to make warships in the 1600s. Then the Acadians settled here in 1782 and have since removed the rest of the forest to make way for farms. Today the spruce trees have overgrown the old homesteads and marsh hawks soar over the old fields looking for meadow voles to feed their young.

In Belle Côte take the shore road down to a small beach on the breakwater. Here you can see fishermen plying their ancient trade and enjoy the small beach behind the fishermen's work houses.

Heading north through Terre Noire you'll see the wave action eating away the soft sandstone shoreline. Bald eagles often perch on these overhanging cliffs looking for fish or sea ducks to eat. Don't be surprised if you see lots of scarecrows in Cap Le Moyne! On your way to St. Joseph du Moine you'll see signs for La Bella Mona Lisa Art Gallery, where you'll find all sorts of wonderful animal folk art. Another good reason for stopping is to ask Michel Williatte-Battet, the artist in residence, for permission to walk his trail to the beach and find great fossils. Look in the dark sandstone rock for ancient petrified fern-like trees.

Stop at the look-off in St. Joseph du Moine and view the valley that lies between the highland and the coast. The valley was probably carved out of gypsum and other soft rocks by the last glacier. Now the valley is home to farmlands, lakes, and small sinkholes. I sometimes find crossbills, finches and deer in this area.

As you cross the bridge at the village of Grand Étang (Big Pond), you'll see lobster and crab boats near the pier. There is a family of river otters in the bay which you can spot quite easily when they come out to play. By turning right at the top of the hill

Woodcut 40" x 25"

onto Carding Mill Road you can explore the low fjord from which the village gets its name. At the back of this saltwater bay, great blue heron roost at night, while during the day the white moon jellyfish ruin my swim.

A very long crescent shaped beach stretches from the mouth of Grand Étang to Chéticamp Island. Near Grand Étang the beach is mostly boulders, rocks and pebbles but because of longshore ocean currents, the sand that is eroded off the bluffs is transported north to the island of Chéticamp, creating sand beaches.

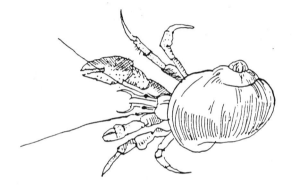

Driving north, make a left turn to Plage Saint–Pierre (St. Pierre Beach). This road to Chéticamp Island was also created by longshore currents with sand from Grand Étang. A trip to the beach here is often rewarding. Children eagerly explore for sea shells, razor clams, sand dollars and seaweed that wash up on the shore. The shallow water warms to 80°F (27°C) in the summer. A small dune system is behind the beach where dune grass snatches sand from the wind and holds it in place with its slender roots. Take your camera. Many colourful flowers are found here: beach pea, sea rocket, sea lungwort, seaside goldenrods, and blue iris. You'll find yourself quietly sunning and taking in the sounds and smells of the seashore. Listen to the sharp-tailed sparrows sing as they fly up, then quickly dive back into the vegetation. During July and August, shore birds migrating from the far north are seen feeding on sand fleas in the beached seaweed.

If you drive past the beach and stop at the southern end of Chéticamp Island (La Pointe), you can walk over to the western side and peer over the edge. Greater black-backed gulls, herring gulls and black guillemots nest on the edge of the cliff which has been formed by the slow erosion of the Island's sandstone.

If you wish to spend more time on the Island, visit La Plage Saint-Pierre Campground which has hook-up and tenting space, a playground for little kids and a tennis court for big ones. There is also a nature trail that crosses the island starting from the campground.

According to Daniel Aucoin, "Chéticamp was visited by European, Basque and other fishermen long before Jacques Cartier discovered Canada. These fishermen used to dry their cod on the shore of La Pointe. However, there was no permanent settlement there before the end of the 18th century. It was also here that the merchant from Jersey Island, Charles Robin, set up his fishing post which attracted the first permanent settlers.

"The first Acadians to settle in Chéticamp in 1782 were Pierre Bois and Joseph Richard. Soon other Acadians arrived, about 20 with families, all victims of the Expulsion of 1755. The list of names of the first settlers, to which others were added later is as follows: Aucoin, Boudreau, Bourgeois, Chiasson, Cormier, Deveau, Doucet, Gaudet, LeBlanc, Maillet, Poirier and Roach."

If you like hospitality, Chéticamp is the place to be. This Acadian village offers you museums, restaurants, lodging, a pharmacy, laundromat, banking and for the naturalist, two different whale cruises, and a deep sea cruise. There is also a small ship that sails round trip to the Magdalen Islands, so if you like, on a side trip you could visit Québec, "la belle province". Behind the village, at the foot of the highlands, there are several local all terrain vehicle (ATV) trails that traverse overgrown fields and evergreen forest.

Petit Étang (Little Pond) lies just outside the entrance to Cape Breton Highlands National Park. Near here is an alkaline marsh with some rare and unusual things like buckthorns, showy lady's slippers, and blue spotted salamanders. The stream running into the marsh meanders through an old gypsum mine which gives the marsh its alkaline nature.

Cape Breton Highlands National Park

When you cross the bridge over the Chéticamp River you enter Cape Breton Highlands National Park. Stop at the Information Centre and get oriented to this wilderness area which was set aside as a National Park in the 1930s. Fishing licenses, vehicle, and camping permits can be purchased in the centre. You'll find a ten minute slide show and friendly helpful staff, plus a nature book store and lots of exhibits. Parts of the main exhibit hall were created especially for hands-on nature games which your kids will enjoy, and you will too, if you still have the kid in you.

The Chéticamp Campground has forested campsites with fire-places, and clearings with power and water for recreational vehicles. The lower campground has an outdoor theatre with nature shows every night throughout the summer. The campground area is a good place to watch perching song birds, especially warblers.

As we travel the Cabot Trail in this book we'll stop and look at every trail along the way. Park your car or bike here for now, as we'll be in the Chéticamp Campground area for many fun filled hours. As for the trails, let's hike them all, but don't forget that in national parks we pack out what we bring in. Let's not leave behind any garbage or remove anything natural.

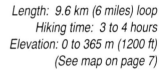

1. L'Acadien Trail
Length: 9.6 km (6 miles) loop
Hiking time: 3 to 4 hours
Elevation: 0 to 365 m (1200 ft)
(See map on page 7)

L'Acadien Trail is a fairly easy hike both up and down. At the top of this trail are some benches and the panoramic views are spectacular. The trail starts in a young softwood stand that was previously logged by the early Acadians. As you climb up the mountain you'll pass through the Acadian Forest type trees which include ash, red maple, mountain maple, beech and oak. Softwoods like white spruce and balsam fir are also mixed in with the hardwoods. There are some lovely small bridges up the trail with rare woodsia ferns clinging to the nearby rocky outcrops.

When you arrive at the area that was either burned or cut by the early Acadians to provide grazing land for their animals, keep an eye out for bears. Hikers sometimes report seeing black bears feeding on the many small strawberries in early summer. I always hear and see many birds on this trail. Some of the most common are Swainson's thrush, dark-eyed juncos and golden-crowned kinglets.

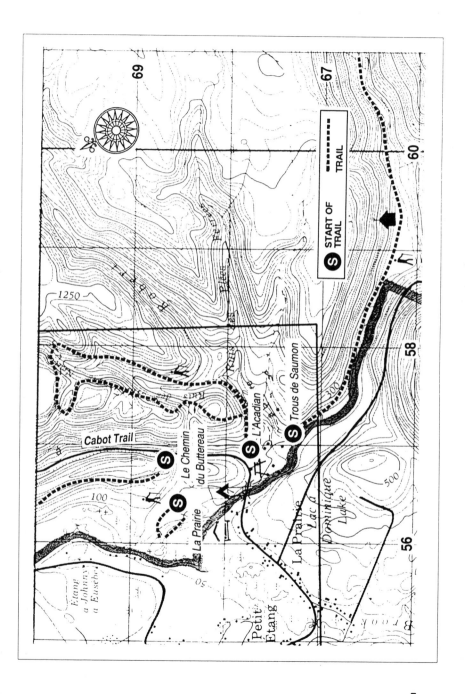

2. Trous de Saumon Trail
Length: 13 km (8 miles) return
Hiking Time: 4 to 5 hours
Elevation: 15 to 75 m (50 to 250 ft)
(See map on page 7)

At Robert Brook Group Campground, a few minutes' walk from the Chéticamp Information Centre, you will find the start of the Trous de Saumon Trail which follows the Chéticamp River upstream. Known as the Salmon Pools, this trail is ideal for a family outing. It's easy to walk to the first pool, 3.6 km up the river. Here an observation area allows you to watch Atlantic salmon swimming below in a deep river pool. If you want to fish you'll need a license and you must use a tied fly in the Chéticamp River.

The trail narrows to a path and continues to Chance Pool, where you can watch fishermen trying their luck. The third pool marks the end of the trail. Some very rare plants are found in this area; butterworts and Chéticamp goldenrods are only a few to look for. Watch the small spotted sandpiper running along the river's edge, bobbing its rear end up and down. It sometimes makes me wonder about our own life and how we often just bob up and down. There are lots of birds along the trail. You'll hear the oven bird's

"teacher-teacher" song. However, most bird calls will be drowned out by the sounds of the river. The Chéticamp River Valley is absolutely great, with steep valley walls rising almost straight up in some places. This is a very wild river when it rains heavily.

3. Le Chemin du Buttereau Trail
Length: 5 km (3 miles) return
Hiking Time: 1.5 to 2 hours
Elevation: 15 to 122 m (50 to 400 ft)
(See map on page 7)

Le Chemin du Buttereau Trail starts at the edge of Melane's Pond near the Chéticamp Campground entrance. This is the original Cabot Trail, first walked by the Acadians, where you can now walk through clumps of spruce trees so thick they form tunnels. Think of the pioneering Acadians as you pass by their old fields and building foundations. There is a resident goshawk along the way; keep a sharp look out and listen, for she will warn you that this is her territory. Also common on this trail are short-tailed shrews. You'll hear them rustling under the leaves, looking for beetles most likely.

4. La Prairie Trail
Length: 1.2 km (3/4 miles) loop
Hiking time: 1/2 hour
Elevation: 15 m (50 ft)
(See map on page 7)

La Prairie Trail starts opposite the outdoor theatre. This area is the flood plain of the Chéticamp River. It was created by river deposits of silt and gravel washed downstream. During the spring, the melting snow causes the river to rise up over its banks, scouring the land and trees with large blocks of floating ice. Look for meadow jumping mice with their long tails. Gaze upward at 200 year old elm trees and take a moment to touch and feel an ironwood tree. There are also lots of birds to be seen along this trail. It's a very pleasant walk during the latter part of the day. You'll see ostrich ferns and sensitive ferns as the late afternoon sun falls onto the forest floor.

That's it for the Chéticamp Campground trails. Returning now to the Cabot Trail we pass through the Rigwash Valley. On your left is Le Buttereau, a sandstone block that rolled off the highlands when they rose up. It's now upside down, meaning the older rock is on top and younger rock is on the bottom. To the right is the Grande Falaise. This huge cliff and Cape Smokey on the east coast are the only two places this ancient granite rock will be seen. The Grande Falaise is a great place for a picnic, with orange hawkweeds and strawberries carpeting the ground. Follow the little stream and you'll find a nice waterfall.

Woodcut 35" x 26"

5. Le Buttereau Trail
Length: 1.9 km (1.2 miles)
Hiking time: 1 hour
Elevation: 0 to 122 m (0 to 400 ft)

Now you are on the old Cabot Trail where Acadian pioneers first tilled the soil many years ago. Wildflowers, trees and shrubs have invaded the old pastures left behind, making it an ideal spot for birds and mammals. Look for blackpoll warblers and fox sparrows that nest among the spruce woods and rose bushes. Here a red fox chasing a varying hare is not an uncommon event.

Stop at the look-off after Le Buttereau and see if you can spot an Atlantic salmon jumping near the mouth of the Chéticamp River. They wait for rainwater to swell the river. As the fresh smells of the river enter the ocean the salmon decide if this is or isn't the entrance to their spawning grounds.

We've been stopping and starting a lot. That's what happens with so many interesting places to see. And this next stop is no exception to the rule. Turn in at the parking lot for Presqu'île Beach. Those two dark pillar rocks are the day roost for cormorants and are made of volcanic basalt. Between them and the adjacent shiny rocks (schists) is a fault. The fault runs under the two little lakes and continues on to the island of Newfoundland.

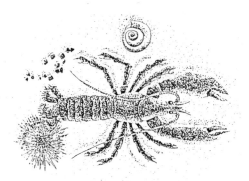

Presqu'île, "almost an island," is another block of sandstone, more evidence of the great geological story of northern Cape Breton. Beavers are in the big lake, coraline algae are in the small lake and rare Hooker's iris is on the edge of the tombolo beach. WARNING ! There's an undertow - swimming could be dangerous.

For our next stop turn onto the La Bloc Beach Road and drive or walk down to the pier. It was a fishing pier used by Acadian fishermen and their families living here during the early years of this century. An abundance of intertidal life clings to the pier's edge. Sea stars, limpets, barnacles and periwinkles are common. Rock crabs scurry about as you splash around. If you wonder why they're so small, it's because the winter ice destroys everything living on the shoreline as it grinds up against the rocks with the coming and going of the tides.

The Cabot Trail now starts climbing, clinging to the mountainside. We'll stop at Corney Brook Campground and maybe camp for the night. A fire and tent near the edge of the ocean can be romantic in calm weather, but something entirely different otherwise. Choose your spot wisely. If you cross the brook and look at the rocks you'll see some which are very deformed (schists and gneiss). There is a lot to see and explore on the soft green headland; bluebells and lots of smells.

6. Corney Brook
Length: 8 km (5 miles)
Hiking time: 2 to 3 hours
Elevation: 0 to 75 m (0 to 250 ft)
(See map on page 14)

Bobcats are reported along the Corney Brook Trail more than other trails in the park. No doubt you'll see garter snakes, our biggest of the four kinds of harmless snakes in Cape Breton. The trail starts across from the parking lot. After a short climb you can look down on a turbulent gorge in the brook. The fuzzy looking shrub behind you is Shepherdia, an unusual plant in Cape Breton.

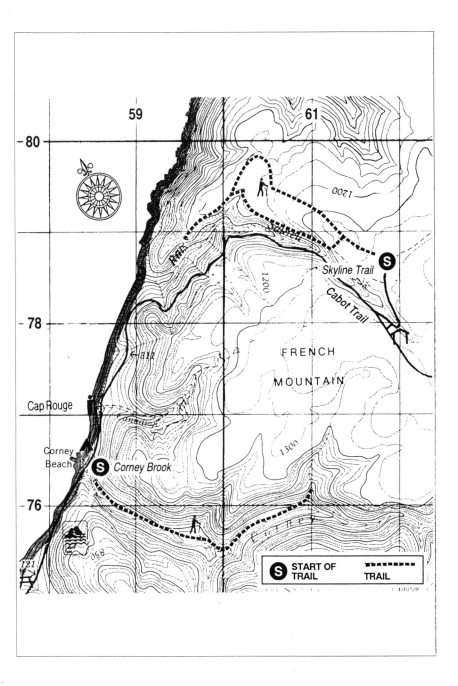

Farther up the trail, stop and look at the hillside that is made up of small rocks and boulders. This talus slope is home to the rare rock vole found only in northern Cape Breton for Nova Scotia. It's a fascinating trail for me, especially hearing the flute-like songs of the Swainson's thrush over and over again. Yes, this certainly is a canyon; a box canyon, with only one way out. But before we leave let's make it to the waterfall at the end of the trail.

Be sure to stop at the next pull-off. The geology exhibit is very good; clear, simple information about the rocks that you see across the way.

A veteran's monument identifies the next look-off, going up the mountain which is famous for whale watching. Black fins moving up and down in the water identify the pilot whales. I have seen minke, humpback and fin back whales here, as well as white-sided dolphins. Other whale watchers have reported the blue whale and sperm whale from this look-off. Large pods of pilot whales, sometimes exceeding 200 animals, are observed here each year.

Now we start to climb French Mountain. All the roadside rocks are bent or twisted or squashed. As we start up the mountain the rocks are younger than the rocks on top. Climbing up the mountain you'll see bolts in the rocks to help hold them in place. Across the valley is the Skyline Ridge. We'll definitely hike that trail; just

turn left at the top of the mountain, and drive along the gravel road for about one kilometre to the Skyline Trail head.

7. Skyline Trail
Length: 7 km (4.3 miles) return
Hiking Time: 2 to 3 hours
Elevation: 320 to 400 m (1050 to 1350 ft)
(See map on page 14)

As you walk along the Skyline Trail keep an eye out for spruce grouse. They are slow and appear to be unaware of our presence. Further along the trail you'll notice that the area looks disturbed, originally because of a forest fire in the 1950s. More recently, during the winter, moose almost kill the trees by browsing as high as they can reach.

What most people really like is the end of the trail. From the vantage point of a headland cliff you can peer down on the Cabot Trail. Turn towards the Gulf of St. Lawrence and watch for pilot

Woodcut 40" x 25"

whales and bald eagles. This is a great place to relax and while you sit here you might discover the rare golden heather. It's quite small, like all the other plants on this windswept headland. If children have joined you on the hike, beware of the dangers of high winds and the cliff edges.

Up here on the highlands the land is more or less flat. The common highland trees are tamarack, black spruce, balsam fir and white birch. As you drive by, take a look at French Lake and see if there are any moose feeding on pond lily roots submerged in the lake.

Our next stop is the pull-off across from the Park's radio transmitter. (It's that rocket-like structure about a kilometre from French Lake.) Here you can see first hand a dry barren area mixed with bogs, typical of the highland plateau. As you leave this parking lot the view of the highlands is a patchwork of trees, barrens and bogs that are characteristic of this poorly drained, harshly weathered environment.

8. Bog Trail

Length: 0.6 km (0.4 miles) loop
Hiking Time: 20 to 30 minutes
Elevation: 410 m (1350 ft)

I highly recommend stopping at the Bog. It's a short self-guiding boardwalk trail through and around a typical late development bog. The stunted black spruce and tamarack, even the tiny ones, are around 50 years old. Pitcher plants, orchids, green frogs and gray-cheeked thrushes are only a few of the lovely plants and animals that live in this highland plateau bog.

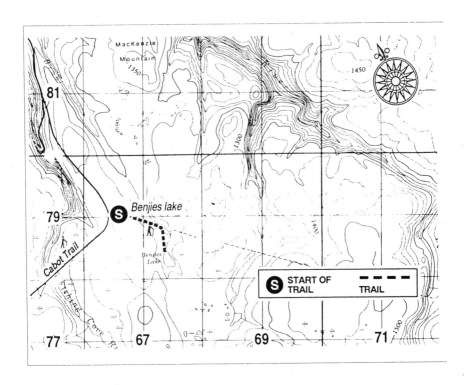

9. Benjies Lake Trail
Length: 3.2 km (2 miles) return
Hiking time: 1 to 2 hours
Elevation: 396 to 400 m (1300 to 1350 ft)
(See map on page 18)

At Benjies Lake you walk through wet barrens and evergreen forest typical of the highland plateau. The trail is in good shape and all along it you can smell twinflowers and many other subtle natural aromas. Schreiber's moss nestles under the yew branches, and they in their turn under balsam fir trees. See if you can spot the pure white Indian pipes and the bright red Amanita mushrooms. It's like another world, on a small scale. The laws of nature are the same here, but they express themselves differently. A small creature like the brown elfin butterfly merely sweeps her wings once and propels herself upwards, quite a distance, before slowly floating back down. Black flies walk upside down on the underside of overhanging bluebeads, defying gravity. If we humans weren't so big we would probably act a lot differently in the same forest.

This is a good trail for seeing shrubs like mountain holly and wintergreen. Watch for big moose tracks everywhere - their droppings tell you how common they are. One evening I was returning home along this trail when I saw a moose headed in my direction. I quickly decided that if I stood behind a large yellow birch tree she wouldn't see me. I then had the idea that perhaps I could reach out and touch her back as she passed (not a good idea!). Just then a little owl saw me being sneaky and dive bombed me, pulling hair right out of my head. The moose, startled by all the commotion, disappeared crashing into the woods. And there in the tree just above my head perched a very brave saw-whet owl. In her talons was one lone hair, evidence that she had been my teacher and protector that evening.

About two thirds of the way along the trail there is a bench in the middle. Turning right here will take us to Benjies Lake. Some sec-

Woodcut 26" x 18"

tions of the route have boardwalk to protect the trail, including the bunchberries and starflowers. Listen for the yellowlegs. A bird that is heard before seen, the yellowleg nests in open bogs around the lake. Lots of people have reported seeing moose in Benjies Lake almost any time of the day or night. Look around the edge of the lake for salamanders and the red-spotted newts that spend most of their lives under the water.

Now let's go back to that bench we passed. If we continue on the trail we'll need a compass, a map and shoes that can get wet and muddy. It's really only difficult trekking for the first little way. You can go all the way to the Mackenzie River along this trail, seeing many things; mink frogs in cold bog ponds, coyotes on the dry rocky barrens, lots of wind and rocks, and vast blue sky.

10. Fishing Cove Trail

Length: 16 km (10 miles)
Hiking Time: 4 to 5 hours
Elevation: 0 to 330 m (0 to 1100 ft)

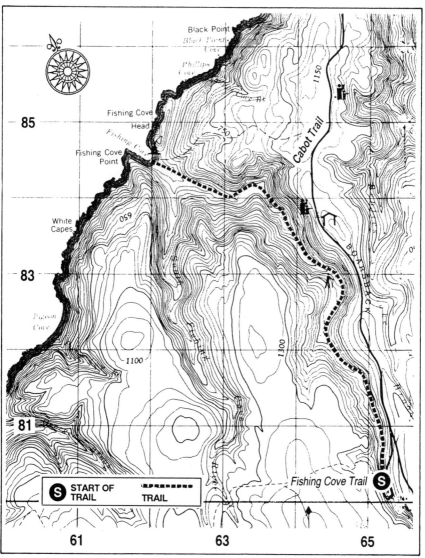

Snake-like, Fishing Cove Trail winds down 1100 feet to the Gulf of St. Lawrence. All along this wild western section of the park you'll notice the forest is different. We see more choke cherries and pin cherries here. Watch the cedar waxwings perching in the mountain ash, sharing the bright red berries among the flock. Black-and-white warblers dart among the evergreens along the way.

One of the two designated wilderness campgrounds in the Park is at the bottom of this trail. This is a popular site so you will have to reserve a campsite by purchasing a permit at one of the main entrances to the park. Pilot whales often swim into the cove here in the summer and the blueberries are unbeatable. As you prowl along the headland looking for black crowberries, see if you can find three-toothed cinquefoil. It is a northern plant. And why shouldn't we find it here, we are in the far north of Cape Breton? When we finish here, let's remember to keep the campground clean. Carry out more than you bring in.

After leaving Fishing Cove Trail head, drive two kilometres and then slowly cross the Boar's Back. This is where the road travels along the top of a narrow ridge with drops of 1100 feet on one side and 600 feet on the other. It is the one place in the park you can gaze down two different river valleys at the same time.

The next pull-off provides a view of Fishing Cove. Smell the fresh air, look down on the wilderness campsite and imagine being there right now.

As the Cabot Trail descends Mackenzie Mountain there are three major information pull-offs. Be sure to stop; the information here is great and the views are spectacular. The forest is very young on Mackenzie Mountain, consisting of small white birch, white spruce and some cherry. A fire in the late 1940s ravaged Mackenzie Mountain and the story of the local residents' peril is told on the third pull-off. This part of the trail is especially fun for sports car drivers and bikers. You round many hairpin turns as you descend to Pleasant Bay, the small village below.

The MacKenzie River is said to be good for trout fishing on the lower reaches. Travelling upriver on foot for one and a half hours you come upon two magnificent waterfalls. Both have deep pools to swim in and usually you will be the only visitors to this paradise.

The small fishing community of Pleasant Bay has restaurants, motels, a small convenience store, a whale art shop, a whale cruise and several sandy beaches. In the village we can leave the Cabot Trail for a side trip. Turn left at the intersection and the road will take you along the coast to Red River and beyond to the start of the Pollett's Cove Trail. The road itself is on an ancient beach which was formed at a time when sea level was much higher than today. I've never seen as many bears in one valley as in Red River. Perhaps the garbage dump in Pleasant Bay has something to do with it. Continue on past Gampo Abbey (a Buddhist monastery) and park at the end of the road.

11. Pollett's Cove Trail

Length: 19 km (11.5 miles) return
Hiking time: 8 hours
Elevation: 0 to 366 m (0 to 1200 ft)
(See map on page 24)

The Pollett's Cove Trail starts after you cross the small bridge and pass the summer cottage. This trail is of medium difficulty and should only be attempted if you are strong and healthy and prepared to wade across streams. There are places to camp in Pollett's Cove. However, since this is private property, we must all keep it clean if we want to use this special area.

As you walk along this trail you will notice some very healthy sugar maple and yellow birch trees. This makes the western coast of the Highlands much more 'southern' looking than the eastern coast. As you go up and down the mountains, chipmunks come out of their hiding places to see the few visitors that pass this way. Perhaps they are hiding from the marten, which is rare now, due probably to trapping pressure. Most people describe this trail as a "beautiful experience". You might find a continuation of the trail

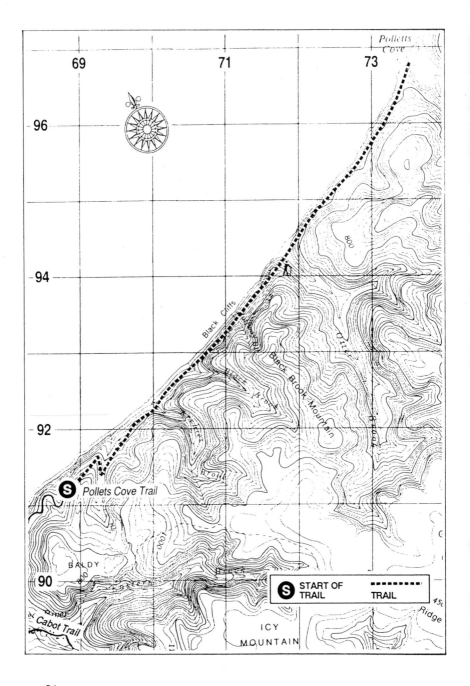

that will take you all the way to Lowland Cove and on to Meat Cove. I have not yet found this trail. Good luck if you try it but be warned that people sometimes get lost attempting this trail. Be prepared to get your feet wet in the bogs on top.

 Back in Pleasant Bay we'll continue on the Cabot Trail as it follows the Grande Anse River to the base of North Mountain. The Grande Anse Valley is full of big hardwoods such as sugar maple, red oak, yellow birch, hemlock and ironwood. A small campground with a shelter and spring water awaits you at MacIntosh Brook. The people of Pleasant Bay have been coming here since their arrival in the 1800s. There was a sawmill here before the Park was established. You might discover it's foundation behind the campground. Perhaps you'll have time to explore the little brook here and its lovely waterfall.

12. MacIntosh Brook
Length: 2.8 km (2 miles)
Hiking time: 50 minutes
Elevation: 30 m (100 ft)

The trail goes up one side of the brook and descends on the other side. Large old hardwoods, with naked miterworts, and many ferns and wood frogs are to be found on the right side, while softwoods, red squirrels and toads are on the left. Hiking across bridges, smelling mayflowers and singing at the falls is all part of the MacIntosh Brook trail experience.

13. Lone Shieling Trail

Length: 0.8 km (1/2 mile)
Hiking time: 15 to 20 minutes
Elevation: 75 m (250 ft)

The Lone Shieling site has a short walk through the edge of a wonderful valley. The old trees here were not cut by the early settlers. Nature continues what she has been doing for the last 10,000 years. This short trail gives you a taste of what this truly primeval forest is like. The purple flowers of the rose twisted stalk enjoy the shade of the towering trees. A few of the rare ferns which are found here are green spleenworts, holly ferns and maidenhair ferns. Red-backed salamanders hide under fallen logs in the daytime and come out only at night, being afraid of almost everyone. Both great horned owls and barred owls hunt the many small rodents that feed on the millions of seeds this forest provides for them.

This valley is a very special place. The trees are the same age and type as they were when John Cabot first arrived. This area is a benchmark for us to gauge what we have done to the rest of Cape Breton's original forest. Spring is the best time to see wildflowers in this forest because later on, after the leaves come out, much less sunshine reaches the forest floor. Violets, spring beauty and nodding trilliums brighten up the floor of this shaded green carpet of young trees and ferns. Our earliest butterflies, mourning cloaks, come out of hibernation, spread their dark, white bordered wings and begin to feed and dance.

As we leave the Lone Shieling we climb up out of the hardwood valley onto the top of North Mountain. Near the top of the mountain you may notice some green coloured rocks on the hillside. This is the only place on the Cabot Trail that you can see the old North American continent, called the Blair River Terrane (1.5 billion years old). The rest of Cape Breton was formed from islands or chips of land off the coasts of other continents which only recently, geologically speaking, slid up onto North America. From the Margaree Valley up to here and continuing on until we reach South Mountain, the bedrock will be of the Aspy Terrane. This was the first of the three island chains that collided with the North American continent so many years ago.

As we near the top of the highlands the hardwood forest of the lowland valleys gives way to the Northern Boreal Forest, due to the cooler temperatures on top. This balsam fir forest is in the process of rejuvenating itself, not by fire, but by insect, as it has so

many times in the past. The spruce budworm, a small moth cater-pillar, eats the forest to death every 70 to 80 years in these high-lands. The caterpillars appear to prefer trees over 40 years of age and thus give the young healthy trees a chance to thrive. It's not very pleasing to our eyes, but it looks great to the moose. Red-backed voles scurry around in the underbrush while the marten, truly in its own habitat, catches a northern flying squirrel, ensur-ing its own survival for another day.

North Mountain is the only natural bridge linking the two major highlands of northern Cape Breton. As such, it is of the greatest importance to the moose and its movement, and to the lynx which does not like contact with humans. The Cabot Trail crosses this bridge and as we drive it, we must be acutely aware of the danger of harming these animals or even ourselves.

Trees that we'll see along the way are balsam fir, black spruce, white spruce, yellow birch, white birch and tamarack. Gray jays, gray-cheeked thrush and black-backed woodpeckers are the birds most adapted to this northern forest.

Following MacGregor's Brook, there is a little pull-off just before we begin to descend North Mountain . You'll find a trail here which leaves the Park boundary after only a few hundred metres and continues, over some very wet ground, for about one kilometre to Fox Lake. This area offers the silence of back country and, like it or not, lots of black flies. Local fishermen come here to get away from it all and to catch a trout for dinner in the small lake. There are some wonderful views of the Aspy Valley below, if you can find a way through the trees to see them.

You might want to use your lowest gear to descend parts of this steep V-shaped valley. About half way down you'll round a curve which has a pull-off and exhibit. Stop here. The exhibit discusses the valley that we will be exploring soon, and the straight steep scarp extending before us. The Aspy fault is a 45 km long escarpment fault and is by far the most spectacular in the Maritimes. The softer sedimentary rocks in the valley eroded over time and now form the beaches and spits of Aspy Bay.

Stop at the next pull-off exhibit and look towards Beulach Ban Falls across the valley. As you gaze up this U-shaped valley you can imagine the glacier that must have been finishing its work here 12,000 years ago. Purple lupine blanket the hillside here, flowering in early summer. Although not native to Cape Breton, lupines are enjoyed by most passers-by.

Slow down to turn onto the small bridge that crosses the North Aspy River. It's a tight turn. Big Intervale Campground is a good place to stop where you can pitch your tent beside the river. There is a cooking shelter and privy toilets. Remember, fly fishing only is the rule for the North Aspy River.

To visit Beulach Ban Falls and to gain access to the Aspy Trail head drive up past the warden's residence across from the Big Intervale Campground. Continue along the gravel road for two kilometres to the picnic area of Beulach Ban Falls. When the red sandstones and conglomerates of the falls were formed, some 300 million years ago, the area was mountainous like today, but with desert-like conditions. You'll see pileated woodpeckers, or their holes, in the big mature white pines of this area.

14. Aspy Trail

Length: 9.6 km (6 miles) return
Hiking time: 2 to 3 hours
Elevation: 60 to 450 m (200 to 1500 ft)

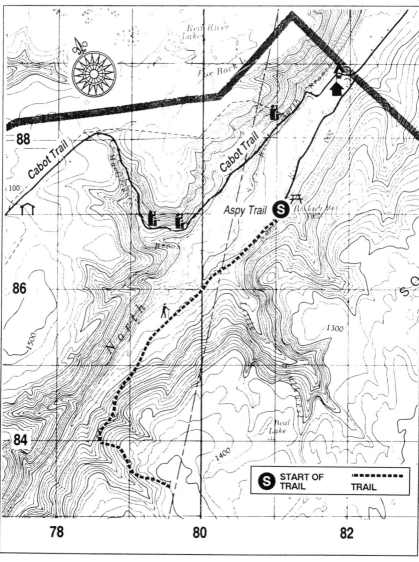

Big white pine trees, old red oak trees and woodland jumping mice are common along the Aspy Trail. The trail is an old fire access road that wanders along the valley floor and hillside, and finally climbs up and up, onto the highlands. Some great views of North Mountain and the plateau can be seen as you climb the hillside. As I recall, red-eyed vireos and dark-eyed juncos are quite common along the lower trail. And as you climb up into the smaller waterways, winter wrens can be heard, but are difficult to see amongst the tangled vegetation.

A walk up the North Aspy River itself is quite rewarding. Giant red oak trees, big boulders in the river, and small pools to refresh yourself in, make this a great hike.

Back on the Cabot Trail, we continue along a ridge that separates the North Aspy and Middle Aspy Rivers. Farms that were

started in the late 1800s are still active today. Watch out for farm animals on the road. This has been their stomping ground for many years so give them the right of way. Three kilometres past the big barn you'll have a great view of the Aspy Valley, its beaches and high mountains. This is the best place to watch the sun rise. Unfortunately, there isn't a proper pull-off, so please use extreme care when stopping here.

Our next stop is Cape North with its restaurants, stores, gas station, motels and museum. The North Highlands Community Museum is small in size but has lots to see. The museum concentrates on the history of the early European settlers in Cape Breton. The memories and artifacts of the Scots who came ashore with almost nothing in the early 1800s are preserved here.

A small village dating back 3,000 years has also been found in the Aspy Valley. It is possibly Maritime Archaic Indian Culture from 3,000-5,000 years ago, or it may have been the Dorset Eskimo 1-700 AD. It's possible that people from all of the different Maritime cultures have lived here in the Aspy Valley at some time in the past. The Dorset Eskimo were followed by the Woodland Indian Culture, and they in turn by the early Mi'Kmaq. It was the offspring of these early Mi'Kmaq people that first saw the white sails of John Cabot's ship sailing by the Aspy Bay some 500 years ago. There is also a 9000 year old site on Ingonish Island.

The Cabot Trail turns right at Cape North, but natural beauty and adventure can also be found in other parts of northern Cape Breton. Let's turn left and drive all the way to Meat Cove, which is literally 'the end of the road' in northern Cape Breton.

High mountains dominate our vision on the way to Meat Cove. The erosion resistant rocks surrounding us look much the same as they did 10,000 years ago, but the vegetation here has changed dramatically. Looking up river from the bridge over the North Aspy River you see farmlands and Acadian Forest bottom land with sugar maple, yellow birch and beech. A catbird meowing may be heard here as well. Now look down river and see the flood plain of the North Aspy River with its willows, grasses, sedges and woodcocks. Great blue herons can be seen flying overhead to and from their colony in North Harbour.

Driving on we are constantly aware of the high mountains to our left. Now let's stop at the Aspy Bay United Church. To our right, behind several trees, is the warm saltwater lagoon of North Harbour with Daisley's Island. When the tide is out, rich mud flats are exposed. These flats are a great place to find green-winged teal, black ducks, various shorebirds, clams and oysters. Osprey and bald eagles fish these warm quiet waters.

Our next stop is Cabot's Landing Provincial Park at the bottom of Wilkie's Sugar Loaf Mountain. The park has a sandy beach, a picnic area and a monument of John Cabot. This is the northern end of a 10 km strip of sandbars, beaches and spits. The mountain behind us is a mass of granite that welled up inside an ancient and possibly very high mountain. Now, the older mountain is gone leaving only the inner granite you see today. Look for a small trail about a kilometre north of Cabot's Landing.

The road leaves the coast and crosses overland through the Bay Road Valley. There are some nice views of the bay as we descend the other side. At St. Margaret Village we can continue straight to Bay St. Lawrence and Deadman's Pond. Here you'll find fishing boats, a great whale cruise and Fred Lawrence's Double Crow, a hand crafted, full size, sailing replica of Joshua Slocum's famous sloop, the "Spray". Slocum, a native of Brier Island, N.S., was the first person to sail alone around the world.

Back at St. Margaret Village, we can continue on to Meat Cove. This area is a hot spot for orchids. Why? Perhaps because the soil is both productive and poor, or perhaps because there are a lot of other lovely flowers in the area. Actually, no one knows why, they are just here. There is also a 45,000 year old bog that has faithfully recorded the temperatures and types of trees in Cape Breton during the ancient past.

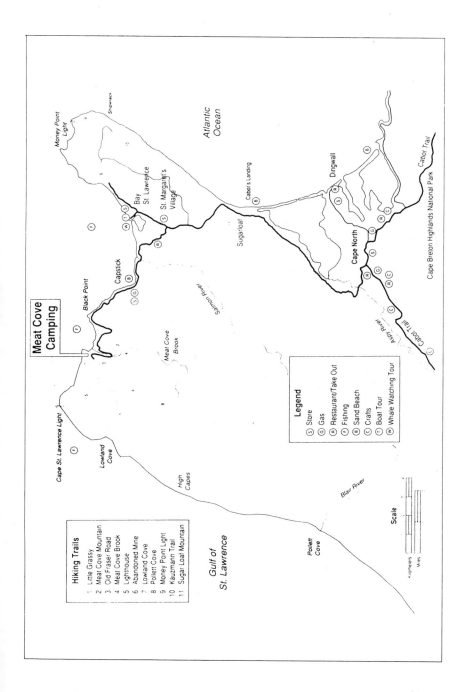

Meat Cove
Camping

Atlantic
Ocean

Money Point
Light

Cabot Trail

Cape Breton Highlands National Park

Dingwall

Cabot's Landing

Cape North

St. Lawrence
Bay

St. Margaret's
Village

Capstick

Black Point

Sugarloaf

Salmon River

Cabot Trail

Aspy River

Cape St. Lawrence Light

Lowland
Cove

Meat Cove
Brook

High
Capes

Legend
Ⓢ Store
Ⓖ Gas
Ⓡ Restaurant/Take Out
Ⓕ Fishing
Ⓑ Sand Beach
Ⓒ Crafts
Ⓣ Boat Tour
Ⓦ Whale Watching Tour

Hiking Trails
1. Little Grassy
2. Meat Cove Mountain
3. Old Fraser Road
4. Meat Cove Brook
5. Lighthouse
6. Abandoned Mine
7. Lowland Cove
8. Pollett Cove
9. Money Point Light
10. Kauzmann Trail
11. Sugar Loaf Mountain

Gulf of
St. Lawrence

Pollett
Cove

Blair River

Scale

Kilometers

Miles

Driving through Capstick and Black Point look for whales. Fin whales, minke whales and pilot whales are common and humpback whales are a regular summer visitor as well. Dennis Cox's whale cruise from Bay St. Lawrence is one of the best ways to experience whale watching first hand from a small boat. Dennis is a Captain who has a great love and compassion for these seagoing visitors to our shores.

Cherry trees and mountain ash line the narrow winding road to Meat Cove. Kenneth MacLellan and family have lived here for six generations and are pleased to offer you a place to camp. They have eighteen campsites in a very rustic and gorgeous setting. Cliffs, seabirds and whales abound in Meat Cove and there are eight trails to help you explore the surroundings.

Leaving the Bay St. Lawrence area, let's return to Cape North. Just past the big red fire hall in Cape North you'll see what looks like a castle made of plaster. In fact, this is gypsum quarried from this area. Long ago (350 million years), this area was a shallow

sea in the middle of all the continents. Salts precipitated out of the seawater and formed gypsum deposits. During the ice age, rivers under the glaciers washed away some of this soft gypsum, creating valleys like the one next to this hillside. Gypsum caverns were also formed that collapse with time and are thus called sinkholes. If you want to see a sinkhole, take the Dingwall turn-off. Drive just a short distance and you'll see a roadside pond. The pond is in a sinkhole.

If you continue on to Dingwall you'll find lodging, an historical boat cruise of Aspy Bay and more whales. The Markland Inn is situated right on the beach. If you stay at the Markland, there's a lot to explore right in front of your cabin. The Dingwall/Cape North area is also a great place to visit during winter. Groomed cross-country ski trails, wilderness, and even snow houses for overnight camping are available here.

Now let's get back to the Cabot Trail. From Dingwall to Effie's Brook the Trail passes some homes and tourist attractions. The forest has a boreal look to it. You would think you were on the highland with all the white birch, spruce and fir in this area. At Effie's Brook, where we re-enter the National Park we can either drive over South Mountain through a wilderness area on the Cabot Trail or we can take the scenic coastal route towards Smelt Brook and New Haven. Let's go both ways: first, the high road.

South Mountain is a massive hump of granite. Starting up the mountain we can see hardwoods, like maple and beech, but as we near the top the forest changes to softwoods, like fir and spruce. To see this a little closer let's turn off the Cabot Trail and drive to Paquette Lake. You'll notice the trees becoming smaller here due to the strong prevailing westerly winds. Shrubs like lambkill, huckleberry, bog laurel and the showy rhodora are all stunted. The hilltops are devoid of forest because of these strong west winds. The John D and Lobster Lake Trail starts here at the lake. Sometimes you can hear green frogs in the lake if it's foggy. Walk up the trail a short distance and take in some really big views.

15. John D and Lobster Lake Trail
Length: 15 km (9 miles) return
Hiking Time: 6 to 7 hours
Elevation: 206 to 460 m (850 to 1500 ft)
(See map on page 39)

The trail starts from the parking area near Paquette Lake. It's a long trail and you'll need rugged shoes that can get wet and muddy. A compass and a map are also essential. This is wilderness and it's easy to wander off the trail and then find it difficult to relocate. Always remember to believe in your compass; it doesn't lie. If you are going to spend the night you must plan ahead and purchase a permit. Okay, let's get going. Hold on! Let's listen for just a minute; we might hear and see an alder flycatcher. They like the wet alder bush areas near Paquette Lake. From their private perch, they fly out after flying insects, then back again for another little song.

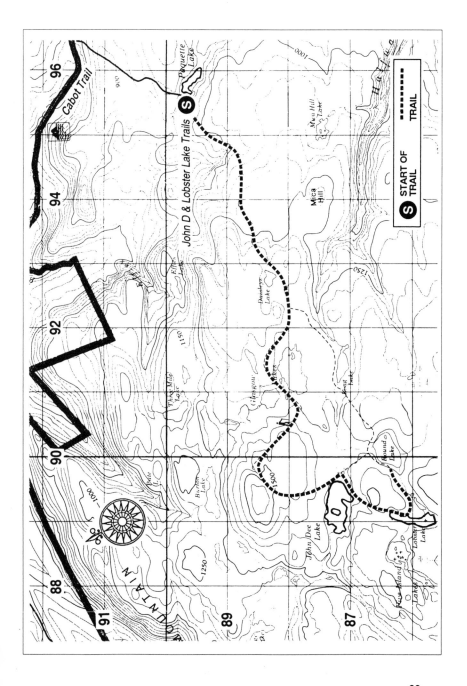

One winter when I was skiing this trail, I followed some strange square shaped prints in the snow. They led to a low branching spruce tree under which a northern flying squirrel had stored a supply of spruce cones. These squirrels live here among the spruce, balsam fir and yellow birch at the beginning of the trail.

Okay, now we'll really get going. The trail starts as an old fire road until we reach Glasgow Lake (3 km from trail head). As we climb up on to the plateau the view stretches northward for miles. Below us is the Aspy Bay, and far to the north is Money Point, the tip of Cape Breton Island. Winter winds blow ice crystals against the shrubs and prevent them from growing taller than the depth of the protective snow cover.

After walking 1.2 km from the trail head we have the option of taking a side trip off trail to Mica Hill. It's on our left in a south-easterly direction. After a short walk (0.7 km) you'll arrive at Mica Hill Lake where you'll be rewarded with great views of the Atlantic Ocean.

Returning to the main trail, continue another kilometre, past small wintergreen plants and cow-wheat flowers to a side trail, on our right. This 2 km trail takes you to Daisley Lake. Along the trail you might find one of our harmless night-time reptiles, the northern ringneck snake. They sometimes rest during the day under the dense huckleberries and bracken ferns. If you're observant you might even find some wild raisins.

Continue on the main trail until the old fire road ends and becomes a trail. Here you can go left or right. Turn right, and soon you'll find Glasgow Lake. Moose like these remote lakes during the summer and you'll have a really good chance of seeing one. Here the trail is sometimes closed due to difficulty finding it further ahead. Now climb up to the top of Glasgow Hill (1500 ft). While climbing, I often see small family groups of boreal chickadees.

Continue down the other side of Glasgow Hill to John D Lake (4.2

km from the trail head). Like the other lakes in this area, John D Lake was created by the last glacier as it clawed the earth many, many years ago. The lake has a white sand beach guarded by swarms of black flies and mosquitoes. Tree swallows skimming the surface of the lake for a drink, quickly scoop up a mouthfull of these bugs to feed their young. The chicks watch from a woodpecker's hole, learning how it's done, and then this new information is strengthened with a mouthful of reward.

Continuing on to Lobster Lake you sometimes have to look hard to find the campsite and trail, between it and Round Lake. No, there never were any lobster in this lake; it's just that you cannot take the sea out of the maritime jargon. You'll pass by interrupted ferns and cinnamon ferns, typical of this wet environment.

Continuing past Round Lake you'll eventually close the loop of the trail, returning near Glasgow Lake. But you might find the going quite hard, as alders have grown over the trail, and you will definitely need your compass here. My advice is to turn back and retrace your steps to Glasgow Lake. From there we'll return to the Cabot Trail. Did you see a black bear? They are regularly seen along this trail when the berries are ripe. So always be aware and let the bears know you're in the area by making a little noise.

Back on the Cabot Trail the roadside is covered with small pink lichens, the occasional wild raisin and, believe it or not, pink lady's slipper. This is true wilderness; lynx and snowshoe hare country. Bogs and barrens are common, as are tamarack and black spruce. Nuthatches and woodpeckers thrive, but the landscape changes in only a few kilometres. Watch closely.

As we climb over the rise to the top of South Mountain and look out over the land to the sea, the forest changes. Hardwoods are mixed in with the northern conifers. Yellow birch grow next to balsam fir. There's a lot of white birch and some sugar maple too. Fire is perhaps responsible for the young age of the trees here. From now on we will see more mixed forest. This mixed forest has mixed birds as well; crows and ravens together.

As we descend South Mountain we arrive in Neil's Harbour, a small fishing village with a picturesque lighthouse and colourful fishing boats. There is a gas station, hospital, store, restaurant and a nice sandy beach. Many of the residing families moved here from Newfoundland in the late 1800s.

Now let's go back to Effie's Brook and drive the 'scenic' route to Neil's Harbour. The road skirts by South Harbour. This is another

warm lagoon where you might see osprey fishing and great blue herons wading. Watch for a small trail leading through the woods down to the beach about 5 km after you leave the Cabot Trail. Here you'll find a 10 km stretch of beaches, sand bars, spits and harbours spanning the Aspy Bay. This is the best beach system around the Cabot Trail. But beware: there is probably more poison ivy here than in all of Cape Breton's few other places.

In Smelt Brook you can rent a bicycle and there isn't too much traffic on this road. Just after you pass Smelt Brook there is a small pull-off on your left, at the top of a small hill. The view here is great. Black Head is just to your left, beyond which can be seen the entire Aspy Bay Beach, and beyond that Wilkie's Sugar Loaf Mountain. On a clear day you can see Money Point at the tip of Cape Breton and St. Paul's Island, 15 miles northeast of Money Point. Terns nest at the back of the beach in South Pond, with gannets diving and whales spouting. This is a wonderful part of the drive.

The forest along this coast is mostly white birch and white spruce. There's wild raisin along the roadside and lots of speckled alder bushes with magnolia warblers flitting about. Perhaps we'll see a blue jay to brighten up our day.

Take the White Point turn off and stop near the pier in White Point. From here you can see graysandstone leaning up against the granite rock which makes up the bulk of South Mountain. This highland granite block appears to have moved vertically upward and to have pushed through the sandstone.

Walk down the little road which becomes a trail to the Tiddles. Please be sure that you haven't blocked the road with your car. Along the way to the cliffs you'll pass many barren spots where only short stunted shrubs like common juniper and three-toothed cinquefoil are found. Look for bluets and the rare purple crowberries. The Tiddles themselves are wonderful. Rocks, boulders and cliffs abound with lots of splashing waves and swirling currents. This is a very dynamic marine area.

From White Point to Neil's Harbour it's much the same coastal forest. Perhaps we'll see a sharp-shinned hawk chasing a chipping sparrow or, if we are really lucky, we may catch a glimpse of a short-tailed weasel. From the little fishing village of Neil's Harbour we can see across the water to the National Park.

Woodcut 34" x 26"

Not far from the Neil's Harbour hospital is the Halfway Brook parking lot. You could start the Coastal Trail from here or, as most people do, pick up the Coastal Trail farther on at Black Brook. Along this stretch of the Cabot Trail in the Park, not only do we see coastal types of trees, but we start to see inland trees as well. Red maple, sugar maple, yellow birch and red oak mingle with the fir, spruce and white birch. The Jigging Cove Lake Trail is a good short walk through this coastal mixture of trees and birds.

16. Jigging Cove Lake and Brook Trails
Length: 7 km (4.5 miles) return
Hiking time: 2 to 2 1/2 hours
Elevation: 15 to 45 m (50 to 150 ft)
(See map on page 47)

At the parking area you'll see sphagnum moss and pale laurel and perhaps a moose hiding among the black spruce trees. It's a short hike to the lake (1 km). As you near the lake pay attention because this is a good spot for nature observations. I have seen mink hunting here for any animals smaller and slower than themselves.

In the spring you'll see many yellow spotted salamander eggs clinging to the reeds just under the water. These are mole sala-

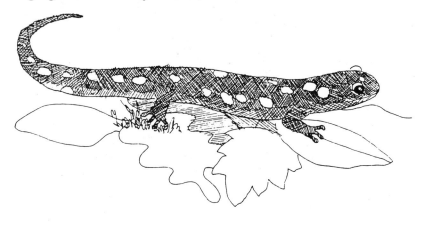

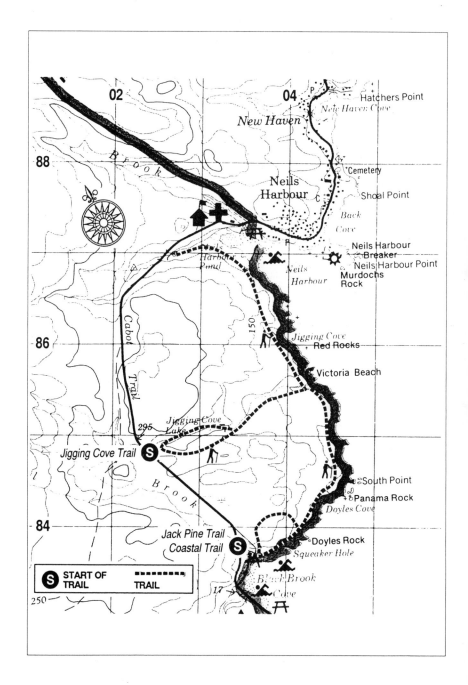

manders which spend most of their time underground, venturing into the water solely to breed. In the shallow areas you'll see small white flowers sticking up in the mud; they are called pipeworts. These flowers are found only on the east coast of North America and western Ireland. Why would this be? How did they get here and when? There is a lot to think about on this quiet, peaceful trail.

Two kilometres from the trail head you'll come to the end of the lake. You can continue around to the other side or take the Brook Trail to the Atlantic Ocean. This is another 3 km return, and you'll see trees like red maple and yellow birch. Listen for the oven birds "teacher-teacher" song, and look for their oven-like nest on the ground. Along the trail's edge is wild sarsaparilla (root beer plant) and perhaps you'll see a predacious rove beetle climbing on a mushroom. Red-backed voles are common in this forest and ravens fly overhead. When returning to the Cabot Trail, I recommend following the other side of the lake or, because the Brook Trail connects with the Coastal Trail, you might want to hike out via the coastal route.

The sea plays a major role in the health of this forest. As we approach Black Brook the wind blows sea salt into the trees, affecting their growth. Twisted and stunted, they continue to live. Let's stop at Black Brook Beach and have a swim in this warm Atlantic cove. The waves are just great for body surfing. A trail climbs the rocky cliffs north of the beach and the Coastal Trail starts just behind the little Still Brook Waterfall. Jack pine, an uncommon tree in Cape Breton, is found not far along the Jack Pine Trail. Both trails start from near the upper parking lot.

17. Coastal Trail

Length: 11 km (6.6 miles) return
Hiking Time: 3 to 4 hours
Elevation: 0 to 30 m (0 to 100 ft)
Access: Starts at upper parking lot at Black Brook Beach.
(See map on page 47)

This is the best coastal trail in the park. The coastal forest is mostly white spruce, black spruce and white birch. Shortly after the trail starts, it splits. To the right, climbing a small set of steps, you have a great view of Black Brook Cove, with perhaps black guillemots floating on the water below.

When we go left we are on the Coastal Trail proper. We'll pass by Squeakers Hole, a narrow cove in the hard granite bedrock. Its unique sound occurs when the waves are just right. All along this trail foxberries and bunchberries grow. Some years the boletus mushrooms are incredibly large. Red squirrels and deer mice feed on them, leaving their small teeth marks in the mushrooms.

After walking 1-1/2 km you will see a small sign, informing us that this is the Jack Pine Trail intersection. After that we reach South Point. The lines in the bedrock are called dikes. They are granite which filled cracks in the original Bras d'Or Terrane as it was pressed over the Aspy Terrane. This probably happened when the continents were coming together 400 million years ago.

Look way out to sea now. Do you see the white birds with black wing tips? These northern gannets are more common during the spring and fall, but there are usually some around, except during the dead of winter. Watch them dive straight into the water for fish.

The trail passes coastal meadows and headlands. American toads hide under the roots of the trees we pass by. Perhaps we'll flush a dark eyed junco from her nest on the ground. If the tide is out, go down to an intertidal pool and see if you can find rock crabs hiding under the brown seaweeds. Or maybe we'll find some barnacles, limpets or the three types of periwinkles. They all are stressed when out of the water, especially if it's a hot day. If you lift any animals off their resting place, please put them in the water afterwards; drying out is a real problem for them.

I always enjoy lying down on the coastal headlands. The smell of crowberries and the beauty of the small blue and yellow eyebright flowers is wonderful. We may see the small crowberry blue butterfly or just bask in the sun. Listen to the waves endlessly lapping the shore marking time on the eternal clock.

Further along we come to the trail intersection for Jigging Cove/ Brook Trail. After that you'll have a close-up look at a barachois beach where white-throated sparrows sing near the coast, but are replaced in the back of the barachois by the Lincoln's sparrow.

Rugged coastline with cobble and boulder beaches can be hard on your legs. Let's sit for a minute and watch for black wolf spiders feeding on flies that roost on the hot boulders. Just behind the cobble beaches are wild roses with Canada burnet. Red fox also frequent this area.

Now the trail turns inland. If you veer to the right you might find your way to Halfway Brook estuary and a sandy beach. Staying on the trail takes you through the woods past hairy woodpeckers tapping out their beat, guiding you on to the Cabot Trail.

18. Jack Pine Trail

Length: 2.8 km (1.7 miles) loop
Hiking Time: 1 hour
Elevation: 30 m (100 ft)
Access: This self guiding trail starts at the
upper parking lot at Black Brook Beach.
(See map on page 47)

The trail starts in a forest of trembling aspen, mixed with spruce and some white pine and then passes by a small stream. Perhaps you'll notice the bedstraw along the way. As the ground becomes dryer we enter the jack pine area. They seem to grow right out of the rocks. Two stands of jack pine are found in the park, but it is rare in the rest of Cape Breton.

Yellow-bellied flycatchers frequent this area for food, then return to their nests on the ground, usually on a mossy mat. Green flowered wintergreen will live here, but most plants don't like the dry, harsh conditions.

The trail meets the Coastal Trail which I recommend you use as a return route, because it is the same time and distance back to your car. Turn right and you'll soon pass Squeaker's Hole where sometimes the water is fun to watch, as it enters and sloshes around violently in this small cove. The coastal route has a coastal forest with red squirrels and sea gulls. There is lots of fun for families on this short trail.

From Black Brook bridge drive 3 km and you will see a small pond separated from the ocean by many medium sized boulders. Called barachois ponds, these unusual water bodies are formed by a stream gradually eroding a small seawater cove at the ocean's

51

edge. A combination of strong ocean waves and longshore ocean currents then begin to deposit sand, gravel and boulders across the mouth of the cove. Finally, as the cove is completely closed off, it fills with fresh water, creating the pond you see today. These ponds are quite common and are periodically swamped by storm waves. See if you can spot some other barachois ponds.

Pull in at Green Cove look-off. Wild roses and bayberry bushes try to stand up to the great Atlantic Ocean's wind and waves. In front of the shrubs are hearty flowers like blue iris and yarrow. The little plant almost in the salt water is seaside plantain. Sometimes I see harbour seals swimming by the cove. They seem curious, and if you wave your arms they come a little closer.

There is a telescope set up at Lakie's Head. Almost every kind of whale has been sighted from this look-off. During the summer, local fishermen catch lobster just offshore. Gannets can be seen diving out at sea and, if you look very closely, you may even see the spout of a sei whale far offshore. It will be a tall, slender blow.

Going over Little Smokey Mountain, you can see the mostly pink granite rock of the Bras d'Or Terrane. Remember, this is the second of three island chains crushed between the continents. From Margaree to South Mountain we were on the Aspy Terrane which was pushed onto the North American continent near the Aspy fault. But that's back-tracking a bit, so let's continue driving on now.

A small but interesting excursion starts when you turn off at Warren Lake. The lake and trail are not far from the turn off. It's freshwater swimming at its finest, with a sandy beach, few people and no motor boats. Try it! Another nice excursion begins by turning up the gravel road to Mary Ann Falls. Driving 7.6 km to the falls you pass the Marrach Group Campground and the trail head for Lake of Island Trail. Along the road coyotes, ruffed grouse and sometimes bobcats are seen. Also, aspen trees become more common. The falls have scoured potholes in the bedrock, so swimming and sunning are popular here in the summer. Keep an eye out for black bears which are known to be in this area.

19. Broad Cove Mountain Trail
Length: 3.2 km (2 miles) return
Hiking Time: 1 1/2 to 2 hours
Elevation: 30 to 180 m (100 to 600 ft)
Access: Parking lot on Warren Lake Road.
(See map on page 54)

It's a real climb up this trail, 500 feet almost straight up, but there are stairs to help in some spots. Blackburnian warblers sing and fly between the mixed trees of red maple, mountain maple, moose maple, balsam fir and spruce. Toads are sometimes seen hiding under the steps. Each resting bench offers well deserved views. As you stop to catch your breath you might notice a small wheel–like spider web amongst the shrubs and herbs. The little orb-weaver responsible is green and thus is called the shamrock spider. Don't worry. It is harmless to humans.

Once, while resting and thinking along this trail (two things that go together well), I noticed a twig on a branch start to move. It was an inch worm on a red maple branch. The birds all missed it, no doubt mistaking it for a twig. Isn't nature intelligent!

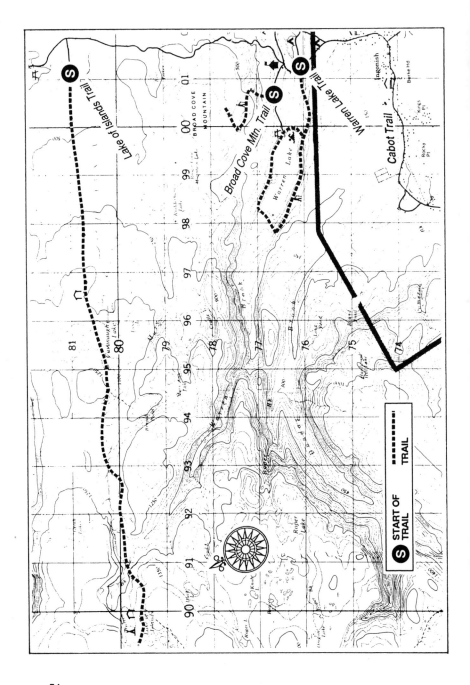

At the top of the mountain the views are grand. You'll see Warren Lake, Broad Cove Campground, Middle Head, the ocean and, to the south, Smokey Mountain. On our way down you'll notice the chewings of deer, moose and snowshoe hare (our only rabbit). The height of the hare chews above the ground can tell you how high the snow was during the winter.

20. Warren Lake Trail

Length: 8.5 km (5.3 miles) loop
Hiking Time: 2 1/2 to 3 hours
Elevation: 15 m (50 ft)
Access: Parking lot at end of Warren Lake Road
or Broad Cove Campground entrance.
(See map on page 54)

If you start this trail from the entrance to the Broad Cove Campground you'll have to add an extra 1.7 km each way. This makes for a good leg stretcher. From the parking lot at Warren Lake we'll walk counter clockwise around the lake. White-tailed deer can be seen in the early morning mist as we start though a

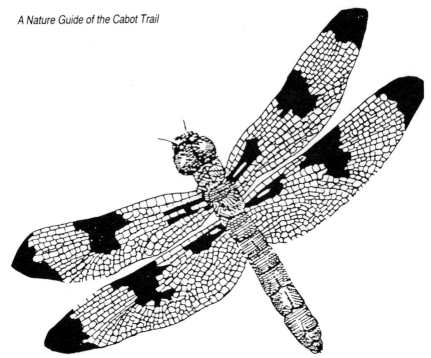

mixed forest with plants like the rattlesnake plantain and agrimony with its yellow flowers.

The forest changes to mostly hardwoods with some large old sugar maple and red oak trees. Look for white-breasted nuthatches working their way down the tree trunks looking for unsuspecting moths. There are many birds here; watch for black-&-white warblers.

There are some old fields regrowing with long grasses. Male ferns might be found near the hardwoods. As you cross the swinging bridge about half way around the trail you'll find pickerel frogs and royal ferns.

It's quiet here. Black ducks, with their broods following, make small ripples in the water as they glide along the grassy edges of the lake. The southern side of the lake is a little wetter in places, and has more softwood trees. You'll discover wood asters on the drier sites and blue flags on the wetter ones. Find yourself a log to sit on and watch the dragonflies catching mosquitoes or the water striders attacking small insects on the water.

Near the end of the trail we'll find a nice sandy beach and good freshwater swimming. The last glacier deposited the sand here at the end of this small, but deep, valley. The water could not escape the sand and this deep freshwater lake is the result. You might find crab spiders in the sand, if you're lucky that is. Cross another small bridge and we're back to the parking lot.

21. Lake of Islands Trail

Length: 25.8 km (16 miles) return
Hiking Time: 8 to 9 hours
Elevation: 100 to 300 m (350 to 1250 ft)
Access: Turn off the Cabot Trail onto Warren Lake Road. Turn right almost immediately after and follow the Mary Ann Falls Road 5.6 km north. Then turn left on Lake of Islands / Branch Pond Road. Continue for another 1 km and park (See map on page 54)

The trail runs thirteen kilometres, mostly uphill, along an old fire road through hardwoods, softwoods, bogs, barrens and boreal forest. This is a trail for back-packing. As we start to climb, we pass patches of hay-scented ferns and then mountain fly honeysuckles, red maple and aspen. Look for leopard frogs along the edges of the roadside while in the lower elevations.

As we continue climbing we'll notice the change in trees from hardwoods to softwoods and finally no trees; they're replaced by huckleberries, leather leaf, and blueberries. About 4 km from the start is a good view point. Lots of sky, shoreline and ocean, which in this case means the possibility of quick weather changes. Be prepared!

Have a rest at the cabin about 6 km from the start. Canada jays might snack on your food while you snooze. You've climbed 1200 feet, can you feel the difference? After another kilometre you'll find a short trail to the left, off the main trail. This goes to Branch Pond, a small trout fishing lake that supplies the water for Mary Ann Falls.

For the next 6 kilometres you should have a compass. It could be wet and foggy over rough ground inter-mixed with dry barrens. You'll see Labrador tea, gold thread and pitcher plants while hearing Tennessee warblers. The fragrant smells will engulf you. Sometimes you might hear some pecking and notice a black-backed woodpecker in the scattered groves of balsam fir, stunted black spruce and tamarack. This is the highland plateau of western Cape Breton.

After completing the first 10 km you'll come to Warren Brook, which flows out of Lake of Islands. Look under some of the rocks in this area to see if you can find the food of the masked shrew, a small mammal that eats things like sowbugs and worms, and possibly even red-backed salamanders.

Eleven kilometres from the start, there is another side trail on our left which goes to Tip Over Lake. We'll continue straight ahead until we reach Lake of Islands. Just before you reach the lake there is a shelter down a small path to the right. Blackpoll warblers might be seen amongst the tangles of spruce. Now get really close and look right into the spruce trees; you may find our prettiest wolf spider, which is dark with a bright yellow band along the length of its body.

Our return is mostly downhill, but it is still another 13 km. While walking back in the twilight you may see the silhouette of a coyote or lynx. Some other day come back this way and see Mary Ann Falls not far from where your car is parked.

Back on the Cabot Trail again, we'll drive just a kilometre and enter the Broad Cove Campground. This is the biggest campground on the Cabot Trail. It has electrical and water hook-ups, outdoor theatre every summer night, and sandy beaches. This is a popular campground. The sun will rise and shine on you while the white-throated sparrow sings you a wake up song. Kingfishers rattle as they fly overhead on their way to a favourite fishing spot.

As we leave the campground we also exit the park temporarily. Arriving in the greater Ingonish area you will find gas stations, stores, a library, beaches, hotels, motels, a golf course, ski lodge, rivers, lakes and trails; the list goes on and on. There are both private and National Park campgrounds nearby. Oh, I almost forgot; there are whale cruises, sail boat trips and fishing on the high seas.

From Ingonish you can see Ingonish Island, where the 9,000 year old prehistoric settlement was discovered. The Ingonish area has a rich history. In 1521 Portuguese seafarers wintered on Ingonish Island. Since then many Europeans have continued coming to this beautiful resort area. You might also enjoy discovering a very talented young artist and his paintings. He is Christopher Gorey and you'll find his art displayed in Lynn's Art Gallery.

On your way through Ingonish Centre notice the tall white pines, relics of the original Acadian Forest of this area. Just as we leave Ingonish Centre you'll see the Park's North Bay Beach access. To the naturalist, North Bay Beach will be much more interesting than the famous swimming beach in the South Bay. Sora rails breed here and if you are present around dusk or dawn you may hear their strange call. The trail heads for Franey Trail and the Clyburn Trail are in this section of the Cabot Trail.

22. Franey Trail

Length: 6.4 km (4 miles) loop
Hiking Time: 3 to 4 hours
Elevation: 120 to 425 m (400 to 1400 ft)
Access: Turn off the Cabot Trail on to the Franey Fire Tower Road.
Drive one kilometre to the parking lot.
(See map on page 61)

We'll be climbing 366 metres in only 4 kilometres, all up hill from here, through mixed forest of white pine, maple, red oak and spruce. Heal-all, a small plant once used to heal our aches and pains, is found along the roadside with overhanging pin cherries

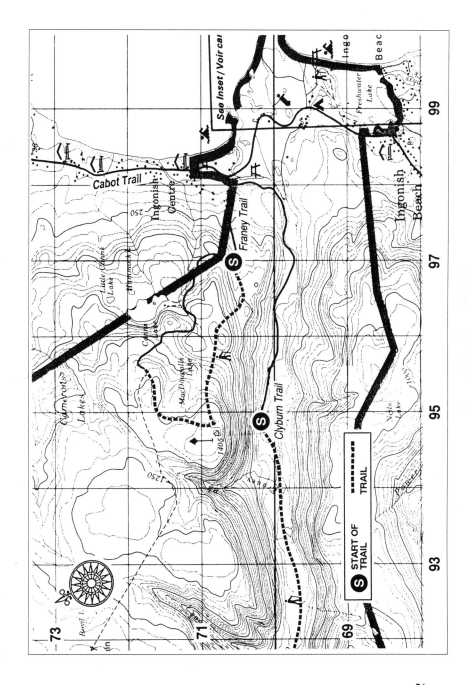

and trembling aspen. After 1.5 km there is a small trail to the left which goes to MacDougall Lake. There are lots of red-spotted newts in the lake and perhaps that's why I sometimes find the red-efts along the Franey Trail.

As we climb and climb, we hear and see magnolia warblers, yellow rumped warblers and of course blue jays. After 4 km we reach the fire tower and there is also a small trail to a look-off. There are some impressive views of Middle Head and Cape Smokey to the east, Money Point to the north, and the Clyburn Valley 400 ft below.

The last 2.4 km of the trail is almost straight down. Use caution because the trail hugs the steep wall of the Clyburn Valley. You'll pass a boggy meadow with greater yellowlegs and common yellow-throats. Red elder and mountain ash are just a few of the many plants of the northern hardwood forest found along this trail.

23. Clyburn Valley Trail

Length: 9.2 km (5.7 miles) return
Hiking Time: 2 to 3 hours
Elevation: 30 m (100 ft)
Access: Turn off the Cabot Trail onto the
Clyburn Valley Road. Parking at end of road.
(See map on page 61)

From the parking lot the old Clyburn Valley Road dwindles and becomes our hiking trail. We'll pass old balsam poplar trees, beaver chews and huge boulders. These giants rolled off the mountain, loosened by chemical processes not commonly seen. Yellow bellied sapsuckers flit between their favourite trees. Beechdrop and coralroot under the beech trees in autumn make this a trail to remember.

After hiking 1.5 km you'll come to the old hotel and storage areas of an abandoned gold mine. It was closed down in 1916 and this is all that is left. A little farther up the trail you can wander off to the right to the area of the gold mine, although there's not much to see. On the main trail things start to pick up, although the trail gets narrower and rougher. You may spot northern parula warblers in the forest and...what's that?! It's the largest moth I've ever seen. These polyhemus moths are light reddish brown in colour with a wing span of 15 cm and big eye spots on their hind wings. All sorts of flying animals live along this trail. Bats are common farther up the trail where the spring flood waters have helped create long shallow ponds that attract insects. Walk past willows and hazel nut shrubs and find the American fly honeysuckles with robber wasps stealing their sweet nectar. What a place!

At the end of the trail (4.1 km) the fishing is said to be good in the Clyburn River but is restricted to fly fishing only. On our way back out see if you can locate a wood frog, or perhaps a barred owl sleeping in a big old elm tree. Both of these animals are common along the Clyburn Valley Trail.

 As we cross the Clyburn River you'll have a good view of the Highland Links, a popular golf course that attracts shorebirds and migrating ducks. Next stop is Ingonish Campground which has shelters and water and is suitable for tenting. It's close to a nice swimming beach, which may be why this campground is full most of the summer.

From here we'll travel out to Middle Head. The provincial government of Nova Scotia runs the Keltic Lodge. It's a first class hotel with great chefs and wonderful views. Middle Head Trail begins at the back parking lot. It's a great experience to walk on the barren headlands. Look for terns nesting on a small island just at the tip of the trail.

24. Middle Head Trail

Length: 4 km (2 1/2 miles)
Hiking Time: 1 1/2 to 2 hours
Elevation: 30 m (100 ft)
Access: Parking lot above the Keltic Lodge.

This beautiful trail, although a great nature and history hike, is not for everyone. The hill on the way back can be a most unpleasant experience for some on a hot day. Otherwise, this is a super nature walk so, let's go.

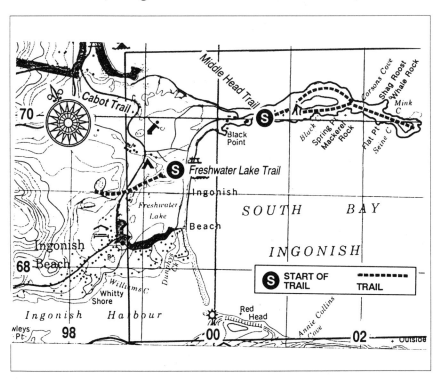

The Corsons, who were friends of Alexander Graham Bell, had their estate here between the 1890s and 1930s. We'll pass along the same trail they strolled on so many years ago, past the same spring, and through old stone gate posts where you can imagine a great iron gate. The trail is shaded by the thick growth of spruce, birch, and some shadbush, its white flowers brightening the trail in the spring. After 1 km the trail forks, the left route returning to Keltic Lodge. Let's continue on to the end before returning to finish the loop.

At the bottom of the hill is the site of an old fishing village active at the turn of the century. It is now the home of meadow voles, active during the day in the grasses. At night they hide under the prickly common and creeping juniper bushes.

Climbing up the other side of this small valley you may find a slate rock on your left. It was carried here by a glacier, deposited, and, after 12,000 years, transformed into a petroglyph by the hand of an early human carver. We'll also pass through a wet coastal spruce forest. The trees at the forest edge are called krummholz because of their snarled and stunted appearance.

Looking out to sea at the end of the trail you'll see black guillemots floating on the water, black-backed and herring gulls gliding over the waves, and maybe even a whale or two. Can you see the little developing sea stack with the terns nesting on it? This special place was not easy to get to. The terns migrate here from the Antarctic, thousands of miles away. Because of humans' inadvertent feeding of the gulls, their population has grown to the point where they threaten this tern colony's existence. Arctic and common terns nest here and in order to reduce the extra pressures from people, the park closes the end of the trail periodically.

Middle Head, made of hard granite, diorite and gabbro has resisted both glaciers and the sea, with her thousand tongues that have licked the rocks smooth for the last 65 million years. The sandy beaches on both sides of this long peninsula took many, many years to develop.

When we're ready to return let's follow the remainder of the loop. Turning right off the main trail we'll see lots of wood ferns as we pass along this cool, shaded, coastal forest. Perhaps we'll find a squirrel eating some gooseberries or startle a deer that is hiding from golfers. It's a little longer if you return by this side route, but the peacefulness of the trail will rejuvenate your spirits like nothing else.

Leaving the Keltic Lodge, let's stop and visit the beach in South Bay. This is what some people refer to as Ingonish Beach, although, in fact, Ingonish Beach is the name of the next small village. You can swim in the ocean or in Freshwater Lake. A walk can be taken along the rocky breakwater that separates Freshwater Lake from the ocean. The lichen on these rocks have a firm hold which the sea can't seem to loosen. Loons calling on a foggy morning is a truly magical experience here. The trail around the lake offers you an excellent chance to see beavers and huge large-toothed poplar trees.

25. Freshwater Lake & Look–Off Trail

Length: 2.5 km (1.5 miles)
Hiking Time: 45 minutes
Elevation: 0 to 30 m (0 to 100 feet)
Access: From Ingonish Beach parking lot.
(See map on page 65)

The trail begins near the small freshwater beach and follows the contours of the lakeshore, which is about three feet above sea level, and was formed from a barachois beach. You will walk under huge white pines and balsam poplar trees. There are loons nesting on the small island in the lake and beaver chews are everywhere. Round-leaved dogwood and red osier line the banks while on the trail you can find prince's pine. As you pass by a small lagoon you

may hear the green frog's banjo-like call. The trail leaves the lake as we near some park houses and we pick up the Look-Off Trail across from the Main Administration Buildings. The Look-Off Trail climbs up a small hill (100 ft).

We pass by red maples, mountain maple and choke cherries on the way up. Herb-Robert, a geranium, is also found along the climb, and then we reach the look-off! There are great views of Freshwater Lake, Smokey Mountain and the park houses. This is the last trail in Cape Breton Highlands National Park.

You'll pass the trail head to many trails in the Ingonish Area but for now we'll exit the park for the last time. Stop at the Information Booth and drop off your back-country camping permits (if you have any).

Pass through Ingonish Beach and down to the flood plain of the Ingonish River. Black ducks and blue-winged teal use the grassy cover to nest in. This magnificent river valley, carved out by glaciers, was once covered with an Acadian forest. Now all you'll see is the odd large elm tree or perhaps a white pine. The oceans of the world have been on a little growth spurt for the last 10,000 years or so. All the oceans of the world are rising by two inches every century, while here in Cape Breton, the island is sinking ten inches per century. Combined, this means the sea level here is rising one foot every hundred years. The Ingonish River's mouth and flood plain are slowly being permanently flooded, as shown by the tree stumps underwater at high tide.

The Cabot Trail winds its way up Smokey Mountain along Red Head Brook. About half way up the mountain, for the delight of your passengers, there is a great view behind you of Middle Head. Red Head Brook probably gets its name from the pinkish-red granite on the top of Smokey. This is the same rock we saw at the Grande Falaise near Chéticamp. These are the only places, anywhere, that this kind of granite is found and its origin is a complete mystery.

Near the summit you can see sandstone rock. This reminds us that the highlands rose up through these sandstones, and that most of the sedimentary rocks that were at one time on the highlands, have long since eroded away.

Upon reaching the top, turn in to Cape Smokey Provincial Park. The views from the look-off are enormous. Across to the southeast you'll see Glace Bay, New Waterford, Spanish Bay, Point Aconi and Kelly's Mountain, with the Bird Islands offshore. On the mountain side the vegetation reveals that a big fire occurred here not long ago. When the forest here is destroyed by a fire or another severe disaster, white birch establishes itself first. These trees love the sun and lack of competition. Not to be outdone, the white spruce of the coastal forest moves in and, after fifty years or so, the spruce tower over the birch, more or less crowding them into a lesser role in the coastal forest.

Looking down the coastline you can see this coastal forest in its natural state. Inland from the coastal forest is what remains of the original Acadian forest of sugar maple, ash, hemlock and white pine. It's not easy to see, as most of this section of the Cabot Trail was heavily logged by the early Europeans for its pine and hardwoods.

The trail from the Cape Smokey parking lot is one of the very best. There's no better view anywhere, but you'll have to work a little bit for it.

26. Cape Smokey Trail

Length: 8 km (5 miles)
Hiking time: 3 hours
Elevation: (600 to 900 feet)
Access: Picnic area of Cape Smokey Provincial Park.
(See map on page 73)

The trail starts by winding through a burnt over area of small birch and cherry trees. You'll find sheep laurel, wild raisin and many mayflowers, Nova Scotia's provincial flower. As the trail descends you'll begin to see British soldiers lichen, starry moss, club moss and a few yellow birch trees intermingled with spruce and fir.

The last glacier dropped the small boulders we see along the trail. Stop at the first look-off with a bench and peer over the edge to see the effects of storms on the steep cliffs. The gray sandstone cliffs are being eroded away. The trail now climbs up a hill and runs across the top of an active slippage caused by the erosion of the sandstone. You will see places where the earth has opened up, forming long trenches. Some day this part of the trail will slip again and rearrange the landscape once more.

The trail continues gently up and down, through original forest of yellow birch, spruce and fir. One 250 year old yellow birch tree, now dead, shows us what the area was like in the past. As well, a thriving 200 year old yellow birch can be seen as we near a small brook.

Moose browses have stunted parts of the birch and cherry forest. Coyotes chase meadow voles in the grassy areas. Hiking along you'll see lungworts on the older trees, some blueberries and wood ferns, and then a bench at the end of the trail. On a clear day, as you look over the cliff's edge, you can see Middle Head, which has a tern colony. Look for Franey Mountain across the way, North and South Bays of Ingonish and to the far north, Money Point. A fantastic view but be careful – just past the marginal wood ferns at your feet is a drop of about 600 feet. Cape Smokey is a great

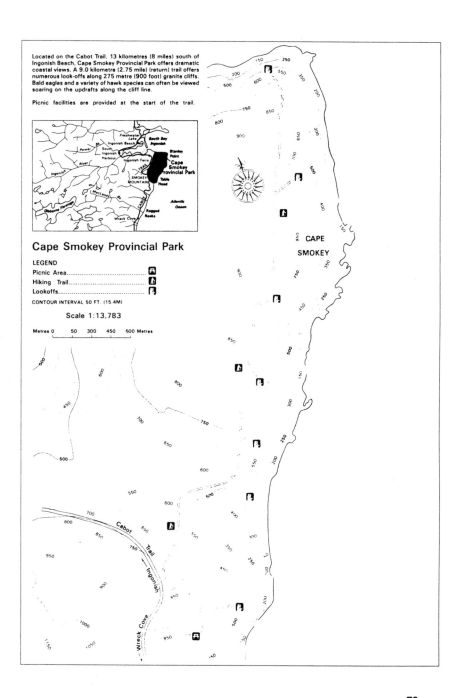

Located on the Cabot Trail, 13 kilometres (8 miles) south of Ingonish Beach, Cape Smokey Provincial Park offers dramatic coastal views. A 9.0 kilometre (2.75 mile) (return) trail offers numerous look-offs along 275 metre (900 foot) granite cliffs. Bald eagles and a variety of hawk species can often be viewed soaring on the updrafts along the cliff line.

Picnic facilities are provided at the start of the trail.

Cape Smokey Provincial Park

LEGEND

Picnic Area... 🏠
Hiking Trail... 🚶
Lookoffs... 🔭

CONTOUR INTERVAL 50 FT. (15.4M)

Scale 1:13,783

Metres 0   50   300   450   600 Metres

CAPE
SMOKEY

hiking trail that often offers a view of bald eagles soaring in the wind.

As we descend the mountain use low gear, as it's steep in places with one very sharp hair-pin curve. Keep an eye on the changing vegetation. First, it's alders and birch, then birch and spruce, and finally, spruce with some birch. You will even see places where the first trees will be large-toothed poplar or trembling aspen, then black and white spruce; a result of fire or logging.

For a side trip you might turn right onto the Wreck Cove Hydro Road, and drive up onto the highlands. The cliffs are great and the clear-cuts serve as a good reminder of how important it is to have National Parks and other protected areas. Warning: there are miles of gravel road to get lost on in this area.

Almost immediately after the Wreck Cove Hydro Road, pull off at the Wreck Cove store and looking northwest over the buildings you'll see a faint green clearing on the top of the mountains. Now imagine being further inland beyond this spot in a blueberry-cranberry patch of unbelievable magnitude. Another one of life's mysteries. Behind the store is Wreck Cove Valley and miles of pumps, reservoirs, aqueducts, flowage systems and dams supporting a hydro-power station.

Driving through Birch Plain makes me wonder when the name will have to be changed; the black and white spruce are multiplying and will crowd out the birch in a few years. The next little

area we pass through is Skir Dhu where you can see the high cliffs and steep valleys that give this area such a rugged look.

As we enter the French River area you'll see the odd white pine tree reaching ten to fifteen feet above the new disturbed forest. For a short scenic excursion off the Cabot Trail turn left at Little River Wharf Road. Very shortly you'll find a little pond behind a barrier beach and a government fishing wharf. Stacked lobster pots, fishermen working on their boats, and great black-backed gulls will greet you.

Next we'll stop and visit Plaster Provincial Park where picnicking, but no camping, is allowed. Buchanan Brook has eaten though the softer gypsum and limestone, creating a passage to the Atlantic Ocean and a small rocky beach. From the beach you can get a closer look at the Bird Islands. With binoculars you might see Atlantic puffins, black-legged kittiwakes, black guillemots or even a razorbill. All of these sea birds nest on these two islands. The island to your left is Ciboux, to your right Hertford. Both are official bird sanctuaries.

While we're on the topic of birds, our next stop is a hot spot. Finding a place to park at MacDonald's Pond isn't easy, but the birding is very rewarding here. The pond is 3 km past Plaster Provincial Park. Hooded mergansers and common goldeneyes nest in cavities found in trees next to the pond. Ring-necked ducks nest in the clumps of sedges and shrubs.

Watch the mothers with their young; it's educational. Bird watching isn't just about ticking names off a list. Watching is a form of witnessing. If we are open to seeing what will happen, it can give us insight. Bird watchers don't want to see what they know, they wish to know what they see. Watching birds, like all nature watching, is a form of viewing reality. Watching little creatures learning from their parents can help us, as parents, to be aware of our own role in our children's lives.

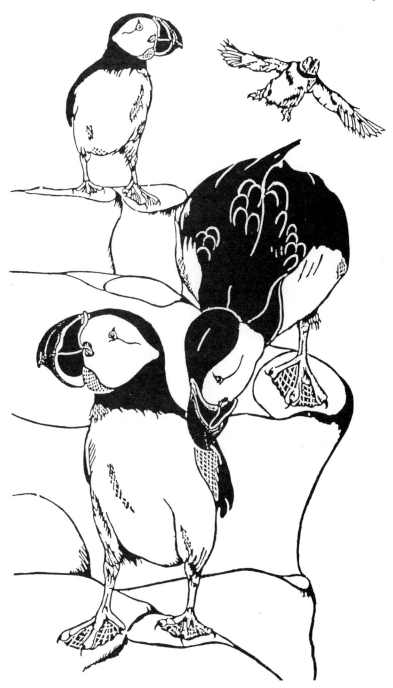

Woodcut 30" x 21"

At Pipers there is a private campground, good food and real Cape Breton hospitality. There are some nice views of Cape Dauphin across St. Ann's Bay. A four kilometre pebble beach starts here and continues to Red Island, but there's not much life on the beach, as it's hard to find a stable rock to hold onto.

The beach is broken only by Indian Brook which is possibly the most interesting river on the Cabot Trail. The river cuts a deep valley out of the hard highlands and is one of the longest rivers in the region. Rare plants like moonworts and sweet-scented water-lily await the botanist. There are several waterfalls on Indian Brook. If you want to explore them, you must hike up the river itself, about 2 km to the Great Falls. Along the next kilometre of river you'll find a group of five small waterfalls called Indian Brook Falls.

As we leave Indian Brook the Cabot Trail hugs the foot of the mountains. In a couple of kilometres we will be turning right at the Barachois River. This fast moving river follows an ancient fault that separated Murray Mountain, to our left, from the rest of the highlands. It's a very magical place down on the river, just over the edge of the road. Minks live in this part of the river, especially in and around the three small waterfalls. There is a dirt and gravel road on the right at Tarbotvale which is good for bicycling. This road forks, and to the right is a bridge and swimming hole, and to the left there are old trees and peaceful surroundings.

Back on the Cabot Trail the main valley opens up to us at Tarbotvale. Here you can see the effects of the last glacier which left humps and bumps on the valley floor. But the really interesting story is that the whole valley, from here to North River, is a graben fault. This means that under the valley floor there is a plate which at one time was at the same elevation as the highlands. The plate faulted and sank downwards leaving the highlands towering along the valley walls.

Driving along the graben fault you'll see farmland along the river and perhaps a kestrel diving or an eagle soaring near the cliffs. Shortly after leaving Tarbot we enter North River Bridge where we have several options. We can turn left on Murray Road and get a close-up look at a flooding river fjord. Strong currents on the incoming tides cause small particles in the water to deposit upstream, creating mud and sand flats. In late summer you might see semipalmated plovers, short-billed dowitchers or sanderling probing these flats for food. Along the roadside to Murray Point you can see the few big white pines that escaped the sails of the early settlers' ships and the chain saws of today. It's thought that this area was a white pine, hemlock, sugar maple and ash hardwood forest with some balsam poplar as well.

Woodcut 26" x 21"

Woodcut 32" x 14"

The second option is to turn right on Oregon Road. Drive 5 km and visit North River Provincial Park and hike the North River Trail. There is no camping here, but picnicking and hiking are great.

Near the picnic area you can explore Little Falls while across the river Spotted Mountain looms. Caution: this side trail to Little Falls is steep and dangerous. This park protects important habitats for plants and animals. Discover deep river pools with salmon, spectacular river canyons with waterfalls, and old growth forest nestled within the steep sided canyon walls.

27. North River Trail
Length: 16 km (9.5 miles)
Hiking time: 7 to 8 hours
Elevation: (200 to 1000 feet)
Access: Turn right off the Cabot Trail onto Oregon Road.
Drive 5 km to North River Provincial Picnic Park
(See map on page 82)

Leaving the parking lot, the North River Trail is a small footpath that climbs 100 feet to an old cart road. Stop here and take note of how the return route is marked (on your way back you could walk by the smaller trail without noticing it). The trail hugs the north side of the valley, high above the river for the next 3 km. You'll cross a wooden bridge over a stream far below. The valley has sugar maple, yellow birch and white birch trees. Sighting raccoon tracks on the trail and hearing ruffed grouse drumming are common experiences along this trail.

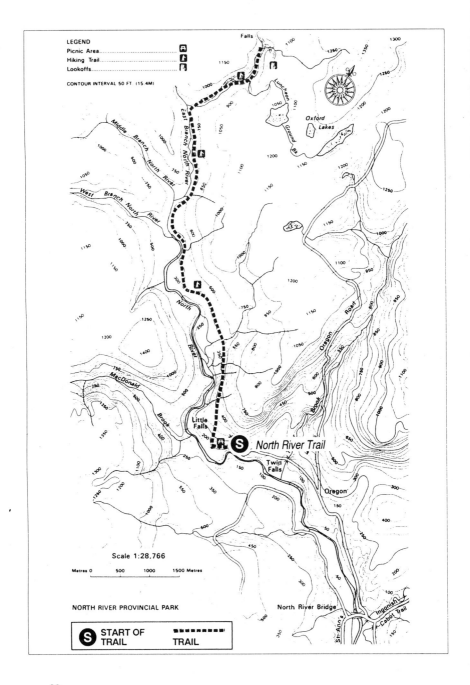

LEGEND

Picnic Area......................................

Hiking Trail......................................

Lookoffs......................................

CONTOUR INTERVAL 50 FT (15.4M)

North River Trail

Scale 1:28,766

Metres 0   500   1000   1500 Metres

NORTH RIVER PROVINCIAL PARK

North River Bridge

S START OF TRAIL   TRAIL

You'll pass through mature stands of hardwoods mixed with some eastern hemlock trees. While visiting the deep swimming holes and wading across streams keep your eyes open – in places it could be rough going. About 7 km along the trail we cross the East Branch of the North River and climb the other side of valley. We cross back over the river after about another kilometre and continue for the final 0.5 km to the falls. The steep valley walls and the thirty-two metre waterfall create a magical setting. A small spur trail climbs up above the falls for another view.

North River Provincial Park offers you this hiking trail and access to a fabulous salmon fishing river, but no camping is allowed at the present time. Don't forget, you'll need to allow 3 to 4 hours hiking time to return from the falls to your car.

Our final option is to continue along the Cabot Trail. Cross the bridge over the North River, and as we drive along, view the river fjord from a higher vantage point. Now we start to see balsam poplar mixed in with the leftovers from loggings of yesteryear. The view from Seymour Point looks across the river to Murray Point and across Goose Cove to Munro's Point where we'll take a hike later. Far across St. Ann's Harbour you can see the Trans-Canada Highway climbing Kelly's Mountain.

Goose Cove might reveal a shore bird if you are driving slowly, or even a Canada goose. You can also see the dam of a beaver family

and their favourite food, alder bushes. For more bicycling fun take the Meadow Road. It's good for bird watching and botanising. Driving from here to Mill Cove the views of St. Ann's Harbour and Kelly's Mountain dominate the landscape. Perhaps you can imagine the harbour when it was full of sails and the French from Fortress Louisbourg were stripping the forest of its big trees. All that remains of the original forest in this area are a few tall trees which were too small to be worthy of cutting at the time of the Louisbourg French.

Soon the landscape changes, becoming more northern looking, as we enter the world of the Gaelic College. This is a good stop. Interested in Scottish history? It's all here in a museum of Scottish and Cape Breton peoples and their ways. There's a lovely little trail going down to MacKillop's Pond. You'll see swallows swooping down over a small barachois pond. There are clear views of the South Gut all the way to the Trans-Canada Highway, our next stop.

The Cabot Trail turns right and becomes the Trans-Canada Highway for the next 5 miles. After driving only 1.5 miles there is an excellent example of a sinkhole, and a gypsum outcrop on the right side of the road. If you are here on a warm rainy night in May, the songs of the spring peepers and wood frogs are almost deafening. During the day this is a nice place to explore for plants. Unfortunately, there is not a safe pull-off for cars, but if you are on a bicycle, go for it.

Keep your eyes open for red-tailed hawks along the next two miles. We will take a short break from the highway and go watch the ocean entering the Bras d'Or Lakes. Turn left towards Big Harbour. It's about 3.8 km in and at the beginning of the road we pass through a black spruce and tamarack forest.

Big Harbour used to be a ferry landing for people crossing to and from Ross Ferry over the fast moving Great Bras d'Or Channel. The current, which changes direction with every tide, moves at a speed of 8 knots when passing through this very narrow and deep channel. Only a small volume of water moves through on any one tide. As a result, the tides in the Bras d'Or Lakes are extremely small, being only 3 inches in Baddeck compared to 3 feet in St. Ann's Bay. Furthermore, this low flow of sea water into the lakes allows the freshwater entering via rivers and precipitation to dilute the seawater by about ten percent. Even so, the lakes still support many marine animals, including lobsters, oysters and seals.

Back on the Trans-Canada Highway travel another 1.8 miles. Take exit 10 onto Route 205 west which is the old Cabot Trail and a very scenic route. On the way to Baddeck, we pass by farms and wood lots until we come to Baddeck Bay. From here the road follows the shore to the town of Baddeck, home of the Alexander Graham Bell National Historic Site.

Driving along this shore you'll notice a high hill across the bay. This is Beinn Bhreagh Mountain which, with its vast estate of the same name, was Mr. Bell's family home while in Canada. As you near Baddeck you'll catch a glimpse of the estate house exposed at the tip of Red Head. This headland is made of pink granite that resisted the power of the glacier that carved out the Bras d'Or Lakes.

Do you see the little white lighthouse on Kidston Island? Well just behind it is the tiny game sanctuary named Pectiale Island. We can even see straight across Great Bras d'Or Lake to Blueberry Barren, high up on the Boisdale Hills. Over 75 pairs of bald eagles nest in the quiet backwaters of the Bras d'Or Lakes. Keep your eyes open; it's almost impossible not to see one in the Baddeck area.

Baddeck has a lot to offer the tired hiker after all we have done during the last few days of tenting. Restaurants, accommodations, sailing, campsites, festivals and musicals are just a few of the things available here. Many artists live in the Baddeck area and you'll find their art in various shops and galleries. The Alexander

Graham Bell National Historic Site has a first class museum which you shouldn't miss. You'll really get to know a different, more personal side of the Bells, and leave with a feeling that Alexander was not that different from the average person, except that he worked endlessly for others. And you'll see the rewards this work gave him and his family, through the exhibits of many of his inventions.

In the small pond just in front of the museum you can find green frogs, our biggest frog in Cape Breton. You'll also hear my favourite bird song, the red-winged blackbird's loud and sweet wake-up call.

Driving through Baddeck you will come to a fork in the road. Continuing straight, up the hill, takes us to the Trans-Canada Highway again and to our next hiking trail, Uisge Ban Falls. Turning left is a more scenic drive which also takes us to the Trans-Canada.

28. Uisge Ban Falls

Length: 7 km (4.3 miles)
Hiking time: 2.5 hours
Elevation: (250 to 650 feet)
Access: Trail is located 14.5 km (9 miles) north of Baddeck.
From Highway 105 take Exit #9.
(See map on page 88)

Long known to the Mi'Kmaq as a special and spiritual power place, this trail is, in my mind, the best for inland highland splendour. Shortly after leaving the parking lot we come to a fork in the trail. To our left is the return section of the Falls Trail, and to our right, the best way to go, is the River Trail. Don't take the shortcut or you will be the one cut short.

The River Trail follows the bank of the North Branch Baddeck River. You'll pass through an area cleared 70 to 80 years ago, and now well on the way to regrowing into a forest. Shortly after passing through this regenerating forest, we enter a more mature forest. You'll see big old white pine trees, 200 year old red maples and some large hemlocks on the other side of the river. The benches along the trail offer you more than just a place to rest. There are river views, small waterfalls and sounds of nature to accompany your rest.

As we leave the river and turn inland, the forest changes and we begin to see 200 year old sugar maples and yellow birch and some beech trees too. Spring beauty and violets are seen in spring, but there is usually too much shade in the summer for most plants to bloom. In the fall coralroot orchids, beechdrops and calico aster can be found flowering.

At the bridge crossing Falls Brook we'll rest. Look at the magnificent yellow birch tree leaning diagonally over the brook. There are mosses growing on the upper trunk and reindeer lichen growing on the moss. Insects live in the lichens and perhaps a spring peeper (tree frog) might occasionally be there too.

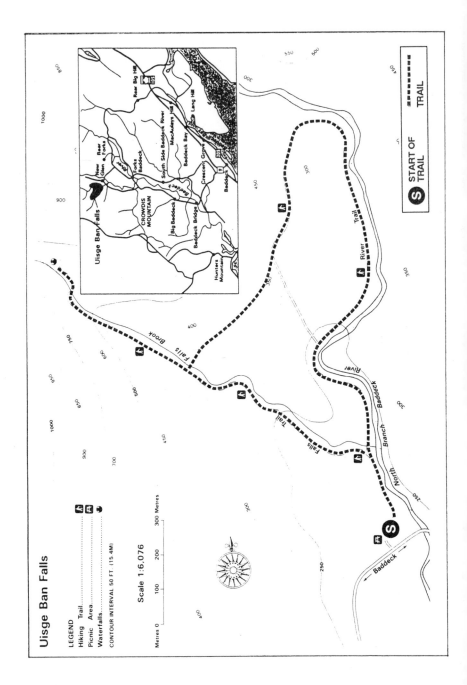

Across the bridge you can see where the brook has changed course during flood waters and has created benches on both banks. From here to the falls look for small pools, rocks covered with rock moss and wood sorrel growing in the moss. You'll see rock polypody ferns, Christmas ferns, holy ferns, and even large old yellow birch trees perched on the boulders along the trail.

At the falls, which is about 50 feet high, you'll feel a coolness and a mistiness that does seem to alter your mood. The mossy steep cliffs (500 feet) on both sides of the brook are home to rare arctic relics; plants of another era. The weeping cliffs near the falls also create an unusual environment where rare grasses can grow.

Return the way we came until you reach the intersection of the River Trail and the Falls Trail. This time we'll continue straight along the Falls Trail to the parking area. Along the way you can see some balsam fir trees that are over 100 years old with wood ferns and steep-moss growing up their trunks. From the parking lot we'll return to the Cabot Trail by retracing our route back.

We'll be on the Trans-Canada until we turn off at Nyanza Bay six miles from Baddeck. If you need any information on fishing, hunting, hiking or hot spots for nature, stop in at the Department

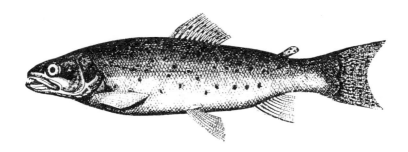

of Natural Resources not far from Baddeck on your right. There are nice views of St. Patrick's Channel from the highway and we'll pass several private campgrounds. There's a really super nature stop where the Baddeck River empties into Nyanza Bay. You'll see a brackish marsh which is rich with wildlife. I have sat here quietly and watched as an osprey dove talons first into the cove and, with beating wings amid a shower of water, rose up, then paused, shaking itself dry, before winging off to its roost clutching a fish lengthwise.

If you have a canoe you are in great luck. Even the novice can paddle six miles up the Baddeck River. The many braided channels make this river perfect for wildlife observations. Cliff swallows veer overhead collecting bugs for their young, while American widgeon forage in the freshwater of the marsh. Eastern wood-peewees, common yellowthroats and yellow warblers go about their day undisturbed by the canoe or you, and blue-winged teal nest in the brackish part of the river estuary. This is a naturalist's paradise.

The Cabot Trail turns inland at the big red barn in Nyanza and passes through both man-made and natural forest. The natural forest consists of hardwoods, like sugar maple, yellow birch, white pine, ash and elm mixed in with softwoods, like spruce and fir. The man-made forest is usually softwoods. We will see these disturbed areas often as we drive this section of the trail. One mile from the red barn you'll notice an osprey's nest on top of a hydro pole to your left.

As we climb Hunter's Mountain we see some farm houses and old fields grown back with white spruce. Yet on the summit it looks more like the highland forest in the National Park. Perhaps there was some sort of disturbance here around seventy years ago.

As we start to descend Hunter's Mountain you can see the Middle River valley below. You'll see the mixed forest and farmlands of Lower Middle River. Far across on the other side of the valley, the mountains are covered with the natural hardwoods. This is the original forest of this region.

Middle River, running south to Great Bras d'Or Lake, has uncovered the remains of a mastodon, reminding us that the world is constantly changing. The weather and forests will not remain the same but will, instead, adjust to the pressures, both natural and man-made, placed upon them.

You can see that in the low lying areas, softwoods have gained the upper hand over the hardwoods. But this upper hand is really the hand of man. The old elm and white pine trees are relics of the original forest, but the red pine you see has been introduced by the local farmers. While driving this area, look for red-tailed hawks and kestrels during the daytime or red fox and barred owls at night.

After you pass the community hall in Middle River you will see an excellent example of a natural softwood forest that vaguely resembles the man-made softwood forest. Black spruce and tamarack form a forest that can handle all the wetness of this poorly drained area. The black spruce has the hump of needle-like leaves at the top, while the tamarack is the softer looking, lighter evergreen tree. Actually, tamaracks are not true evergreens, like the spruce, because they lose their small needles every fall. See if you can spot a rusty blackbird in this cold, water laden habitat.

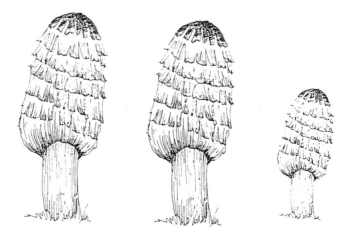

Woodcut 25" x 13"

Continue driving through a mixture of forest and farms to Lake O'Law. Just before reaching the first lake we start to see the mountains rise up and surround us. The water drainage changes course here and these lakes run into the Gulf of St. Lawrence.

The provincial government has established a picnic park on the shores of Lake O'Law. See if you can spot the common merganser and her brood of chicks swimming on the lake. The park is a nice quiet spot for bird watching. You will also find a private campground and restaurant in the Lake O'Law area.

As we continue our drive down into the Margaree Valley we pass several small intervales where the soil is fertile and a farmer has cleared the land to grow hay. White-tailed deer take advantage of this and use these fields at night for browsing.

If you would like some fine dining turn right off the Cabot Trail onto Egypt Road. You'll drive through beautiful hilly countryside that reminds me of the Trossachs Mountains in Scotland; up and down hill and dale for two miles to a fine old rustic Scottish country inn. The Normaway Inn has the finest of foods with a wonderful staff, and if you are the right person this is definitely the right place to stay.

Continuing on the Cabot Trail we soon come to Northeast Margaree where there is the Heritage Museum on the main road. To go to the Salmon Fishing Museum turn right at Northeast Margaree, turn left after 0.5 km, and drive for a further 0.5 km to the museum. Another interesting side trip is to the Salmon Interpretation Centre. After turning right on the Northeast Margaree Road, continue for 7 km past Margaree Valley towards Kingross and you will see signs for the Centre.

The Margaree Valley is surrounded by the highlands and was formed by ancient faulting in the earth's crust which gradually pushed up the resistant hard rock mountains. Far back in the valley, near the Salmon Interpretation Centre, you'll find several trails leading to waterfalls. They are on private land so you need to ask local folks for directions. If you drive even further back into the valley you'll see a large hump right in the middle of the valley. This is called Sugarloaf Mountain and it's made of granite. Unlike the other mountains here, it rose to the surface as molten rock. Behind Sugarloaf Mountain, in Big Intervale, there is a country lodge which is used by fishermen and nature lovers.

Back on the Cabot Trail continue past more intervales and farmlands, and just before reaching Margaree Forks there is an alternate route down to the right, crossing the river. This is a small country road with narrow one-lane iron bridges. It passes the farms and flood plain of the Margaree River along its north bank until it meets the Gulf of St. Lawrence eight miles from here.

In Margaree Forks we find an information centre, lodging, stores, gas, golf, a library and a most unusual store called "Myles From Nowhere". It is also here that the Southwest Margaree River joins with the Northeast Margaree River and their combined flooding forms a large fertile flood plain.

From here until we reach the Gulf of St. Lawrence we'll pass farms, fields, mountains, and rivers. Listen for bobolink songs and red-tailed hawk screams. If it's warm, maybe we'll venture down to the river, finding a spot where the wind blows the grass every which way. And as the grass sweeps from one side to the other you'll feel as if you can almost see the wind itself. Now the only thing missing is a turtle.

Turtles are actually quite scarce in these parts. If you see one it was probably put there for you to see. Check out the complete reptile and amphibian story in the next section of this book. Raccoon tracks in the mud or muskrat diggings in the river bank are what you will probably see. And lots of salmon fishermen in the river, from dawn to dusk. Black flies? Just enough. In the spring this is one of the only places we see bloodroot flowers. In some places they carpet the valley floor when no other life appears to be awake.

All along the river you can see bald eagles as they fish for salmon. When you come to a view of the whole flood plain, just imagine the water it would take to cover everything on the lower valley floor. This quiet, peaceful river becomes mad and restless in the spring, snaking around, creating new islands and erasing old ones. Sometimes an old elm tree, left standing in the water, is all that remains of a small island.

The Cabot Trail crosses the Margaree over a long bridge near the river's mouth. Salmon run up the river mostly in the fall but a few are seen year round. Fishing for this 'king' of fish is an annual event for many fishermen worldwide. Canoeing up or down much of this slow moving river is a pleasant and leisurely experience for a novice canoe handler.

Woodcut 26" x 19"

You'll even find Farley Mowat's 'Boat That Wouldn't Float' docked on a hill over-looking the bridge. A bagpiper beckons you to learn more about the Scottish culture, have tea and scones, rest and reflect on the Celtic roots of the people of Cape Breton. Deep sea charter boats are also available here in Margaree Harbour.

Well, that's it for the Cabot Trail and all its hiking trails, but-there is a lot more to the story. You will meet some of the residents of Cape Breton while on your tour: Acadians who sought refuge here, or perhaps Mi'Kmaq, the aboriginal inhabitants of Cape Breton. Bagpipes resonating in the highlands, ceilidhs and tartans remind us that many Cape Bretoners have their family roots in Scotland. French, Irish, German, English and many others make up the mosaic of life found today around the Cabot Trail.

The people of the Island come from many different back-grounds, yet they all have some things in common. They love music, nature, fresh air and socials of all sorts. There is a saying in Cape Breton and it goes like this, "Everyone who visits Cape Breton always returns again." I hope that your memories will be fond ones and that this book will add to your experience of our land and our people.

Thanks for joining me and remember, of all the things that visi-tors take away from Cape Breton, the magic found in the high-lands, the people, and the forest remains. We all feel the magic but we can only breathe it into our lungs, then give it back. It remains for all of nature to share.

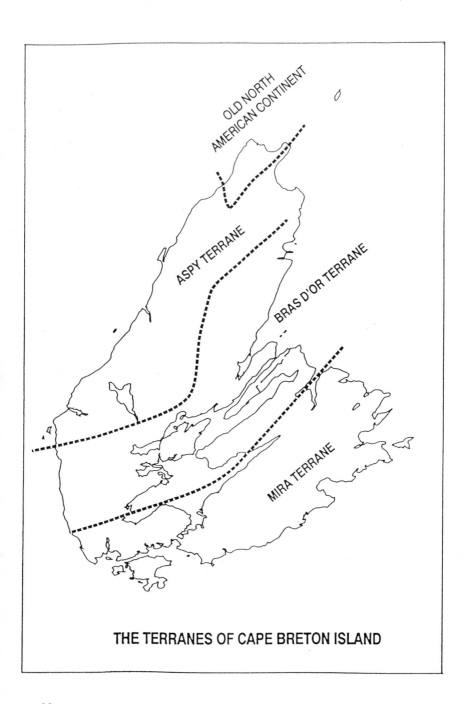

THE TERRANES OF CAPE BRETON ISLAND

GEOLOGY
What We Think Happened and Why

Geology, the study of the Earth, is the lever that has opened the eyes of many naturalists to the complexity and huge time frames involved in nature. The knowledge that comes from this field of study has undoubtedly changed our society, so let's take a look at it.

Knowledge is one of those things that changes periodically. We used to think that the rising and setting Sun revolved around the Earth. Now we know that this illusion is due to the Earth turning on its axis. The information about our geological history in this section is not carved in stone either, so to speak. No one knows the truth about these matters, but after reading and thinking about geology, here is my interpretation of the last 4.5 billion years of our history. Relax! It might all be true, but then again, it might not. As I said, no one knows for sure.

Just before we start, let's reflect on why it is even possible to tell this story. We don't often think about sub-atomic particles and what makes them tick when studying nature, but why not? It is thought that all of nature, from the creation of the universe to the blossoming of a flower, is regulated by certain laws.

A planet's ability to have long term geological activity is a result of the ratio between the electromagnetic and gravitational forces as they interact. This ratio determines whether or not sub-atomic particles can dance around freely and give rise to complex molecules. On the Moon, Mercury and Mars, their smaller size (compared to Earth) produces a greater electromagnetic force than gravitational. The molecules stick together and require an external force to move them. Because the Moon's inner heat was used up early in its development (after 1 billion years), there has been little geological activity since that time.

Planets like Jupiter and Saturn are much larger (compared to Earth) and the gravitational force is greater than the electromagnetic force. This change in the ratio of the two forces allows only a few gasses to survive the great gravitational pressure. Thus, there is no long term geological activity and not many complex molecules. The Earth, however, is just the right size. The ratio between these two powerful forces allows the inside of the Earth to remain molten, a state resulting from the gift we received from the Sun (radioactivity). This molten rock, which the continents float on, has currents much like the ocean, which cause the continents to drift around, colliding with one another and creating new complexity. Most chemical creativity takes place on the surface of our planet. This is where the fabric of life is produced, for all living things are clothed in complexity.

As you can see, the reason we have long term geological activity, complex molecules and life is primarily because of the size of our planet. Of course when speaking of life, one of those magical things we don't fully understand, the Sun and other universal factors are no doubt big players. Yet, without complex chemical and molecular bodies it would be hard to find life.

So here is my interpretation. The Earth is thought to be about the same age as our Sun, the other eight planets, and the solar system – 4.5 billion years old. The Milky Way Galaxy that we orbit is possibly some 12 billion years or more in age.

For the first billion years of Earth's history, it appears nothing survived to tell us what happened. Then rocks started to form that have survived until today, giving us a few clues about our past. It was at this early time that most of the water came out of the earth and formed our oceans. The oldest rocks with fossils date back 3 billion years and have evidence of bacteria in them. What the continents were doing is a complete mystery for most of our history, but you would think a lot has happened since the beginning.

The first rocks with fossil fungi date back 2 billion years. Oxygen formed in the atmosphere and cells with nuclei were preserved. A billion years later, green algae were trapped in rock.

Some of the rocks in Cape Breton date back to this time. They were part of the old North American continent and jutted out into the pre–Atlantic Ocean. Fossil animals followed, having been found in rock 700 million years old. These animals were marine dwelling invertebrates; worm and jellyfish-like creatures. As you can see, our knowledge of this 4 billion year period is not extensive.

Around the time that plants and animals started crawling out of the sea and onto the land (440 million years ago), all the continents started to drift together to form a mega continent. With the closing of this earlier ocean, sediments lying far offshore, so thick that they formed rocks, were forced onto the jutting extension of the North American continent. These rocks are now called the Aspy Terrane which, along with two island chains off the coasts of Africa and South America, were squeezed together between Africa, South America and Europe. These different rock groups formed the land mass which today is the island of Cape Breton. We were in the centre of a huge continent, somewhere near the equator. This massive continent stayed together for an entire trip around the galaxy (220 million years).

During the last 440 million years of our geological history rocks from around the world have recorded some interesting things as follows:

Millions of years ago
400:    first land plants
370:    first amphibians
320:    coal forest dominates
286:    dinosaur, mammal, turtle, crocodile, frog fossils
220:    started the most recent orbit around the Milky Way;
        Atlantic Ocean starts to open
208:    bird fossils were preserved
144:    dinosaurs die out; first snakes
66:     owls, shrews, and mammals flourish;
        highlands rise up from sea level

58:     dog, cat, rabbit, horse, elephant fossils
37:     deer, monkey, pig fossils
24:     mice, rat, and new mammal fossils
5:      cattle and sheep fossils

The terranes making up Cape Breton are shown in the map on page ninety-eight (98). One terrane after another was forced over the previous one. This caused great pressure and heat, and the rocks were twisted and changed, or metamorphosed, because of these pressures. The rock in the Aspy Terrane is thought to have been pressed more than 20 km below the surface. The Bras d'Or Terrane, when it came on board, forced great upwellings of molten rock to form granite mountains (an example is South Mountain). Many mountains have come and gone, covering the island with thick sediments. Shallow seas also left their deposits and in time they too were eroded away.

North America started drifting north as the present day Atlantic Ocean started to open up. Temperatures changed over time and the plants and animals adapted to these changes. Glaciers advanced again and again, driving out the animals and plants, and washing away previous sediments. This continues today, as in the past, at a very slow pace.

WEATHER AND CLIMATE

Climate and weather are the most important ingredients that affect where plants and, in turn, animals can live. Yet most of us understand very little about them. First let's review what it is that creates and maintains weather.

Very briefly, light produced by hydrogen changing to helium on the sun radiates outward in all directions. This light, in the form of waves or rays or particles (different people use different words), penetrates the earth's atmosphere and bombards the globe as it turns on its axis.

As most of our planet's surface is water, most of the sun's energy as heat is absorbed or reflected by the oceans of the world. With the turning of the planet on its axis, coupled with 3.5 billion years of practice, the oceans have developed relatively stable global currents. These currents, which are distributing the sun's heat around the world, also help to create the wind.

Wind is, in a poetic but accurate way, the sky massaging the earth and her seas. The trade winds that brought the Europeans to our shores were, and still are, part of this global heat distribution system. It works something like this. The sky is not just empty space. It's full of many different sizes and shapes of molecules and particles. Some air is lighter than other air. Warm light air rises, causing colder heavy air to move in and replace it. When air moves like this it is called wind.

Because the distribution of heat through oceanic currents has become more or less stable with time, the trade winds are also more or less stable. When warmer moist air moves into the Maritimes it changes the local air temperature and creates conditions which cause the moisture in the air to fall to the earth. Where cold northern air meets warm southern air a front is formed. The two air masses slide over one another creating strong winds.

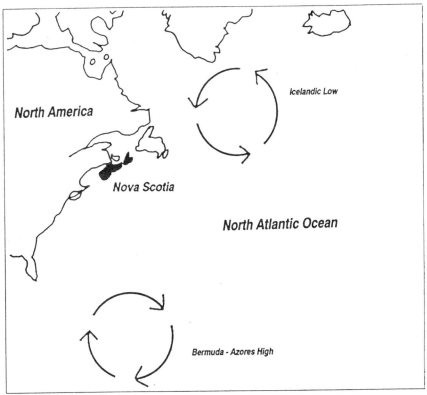

If you are an animal or plant down here under the great sun and sky, weather takes on a different meaning. It is what we actually experience; things like snow, wind, heat, cold, rain and fog. We also experience spring, summer, fall and winter. So what is climate?

Climate is something we don't experience per se. When we record the weather day after day, year after year, we notice patterns that develop in our data. If we live long enough these patterns are made evident to us through personal experience. As an example, Fundy National Park has a foggy climate. But if you are in Fundy right now reading this book, and it isn't foggy, you will understand how we don't feel climate, rather, we feel weather. Ask the old fisherman on the pier and he will say, "You have to go look outside to see what the weather's like."

On the map to your left (page 104), you will see two large vortexes. The Icelandic Low is in the north, with winds moving in a counter-clockwise direction. Cold north winds blow when this massive low pressure system dominates the region. The Bermuda-Azores High moves in a clockwise direction, bringing warm winds from southern waters. Hurricane force winds that lash the coastal area from Chéticamp to Bay St. Lawrence come from this powerhouse in the south.

You may experience different weather in the same day driving the Cabot Trail. Here are some of the conditions we experience in Cape Breton:

Precipitation:	1500 mm/yr
Rainfall:	1100 mm/yr
Snowfall:	400 cm/yr
High air temperature:	35°C summer
Low air temperature:	-28°C winter

The climate of the Cabot Trail can be severe because of the northern location, the elevated highlands and the effects of the cold Labrador Current and the Gulf of St. Lawrence. Continental winds give us cold winters and warm summers, but lingering ice from the Gulf produces cool to cold springs. Warm fall days with the hardwoods changing colour will greet you during Cape Breton's autumn season.

Woodcut 28" x 21"

INTRODUCING THE ANIMALS OF THE CABOT TRAIL

During the last glaciation all of the plants and animals that lived on Cape Breton were forced to leave the island, and little else survived. As the plants slowly returned, the animals that lived with these plants also migrated back to Cape Breton Island. Remember, this was occurring while the ice sheet was still retreating northwards and there was much ocean water tied up as ice. As a result, many of these plants and animals came back to Cape Breton before it was an island. The water surrounding what was to become an island was mostly freshwater melting from the ice nearby. Certain freshwater animals such as fish, northern frogs, salamanders and snakes gained access to the emerging island at this time.

Other animals, feeding on the plants that were following the retreat of the ice sheet, and those following as meat-eating predators, also gained access to Cape Breton. Birds, many insects and some plants came with the wind, and some came on the backs of others. Finally, the last wave of mammals arrived: the white-tailed deer, coyotes, bobcats, groundhogs, raccoons, porcupines and skunks. Even as we speak, the groundhogs, porcupines and skunks really don't have a good foothold yet.

In this book we'll discuss all of northern Cape Breton's mammals from bats to whales. We'll do the same for all the birds, amphibians and reptiles. You'll find a list of the many different classes of insects, along with some general insect information. Spiders, mites, ticks and butterflies are given special attention. Finally, fish are mentioned, while worms, snails and micro-organisms are discussed together.

These lists include only those animals that have been found to date. If you find anything rare or anything not on these lists, please report your sighting to the Provincial Natural History Museum or Cape Breton Highlands National Park.

MAMMALS OF NORTHERN CAPE BRETON

MAMMAL	COMMENTS
Shrew *Sorex cinereus*	Active year round, eating insects, salamanders, young mice, worms and sowbugs. Commonly found in most habitats.
Pygmy Shrew *Microsorex hoyi*	The smallest mammal in the New World is found living near bogs and meadows in the northern forest of balsam fir and white birch. It is uncommon and found in few locations.
Gaspé Shrew *Sorex gaspensis*	This rare and vulnerable animal is found only near rocky talus slopes with streams, and in hardwood forests.
Water Shrew *Sorex palustris*	Uncommon. Found along streamside locations or near running water. Shrews destroy large numbers of insect larvae. Their strong smell is for protection from predators.
Short-tailed Shrew *Blarina brevicauda*	Very noisy. Commonly found in hardwood forests and grassy meadows. They eat other shrews and meadow voles, as well as the usual insect diet.
Star-nosed Mole *Condylura cristata*	They are common locally in suitable lowlands, usually near water, and they are good swimmers. They make mole hills and tunnels, and eat

aquatic insects, worms and leeches. They are strong smelling for protection from predators.

Little Brown Bat
Myotis lucifugus

Uncommon in river valleys, this bat roosts in caves, old mines, hollow trees and buildings. Hibernates.

Northern Long-eared Bat
Myotis septentrionalis

Probably common throughout northern Cape Breton. Its large ears help to identify it from the little brown bat. It is known to hibernate all winter in mainland Nova Scotia.

Red Bat
Lasiurus borealis

Although none have been detected in our area to date, this migrating red coloured bat may live in Cape Breton in small numbers.

Hoary Bat
Lasiurus cinereus

The hoary bat is uncommon, and migrates south for the winter. It is active during the hours of darkness, as are all bats found in Cape Breton.

Silver-haired Bat
Lasionycteris noctivagans

One sighting and photograph of the silver–haired bat, our largest, was reported by Britt Roscoe of Baddeck.

Deer Mouse
Peromyscus maniculatus

Common throughout the island, they are active at night. Deer mice have big eyes and large ears to help protect themselves from predators.

House Mouse
Mus domesticus

Introduced and rarely found in Cape Breton towns. The deer mouse is more common in Cabot Trail homes than the house mouse.

Red-backed Vole
Clethrionomy gapperi

Common throughout most forest habitats, these voles are nervous, active day or night, and do not store food. They prefer evergreen forests with small streams.

Meadow Vole
Microtus pennsylvanicus

Uncommon; found in grasslands and marshes. Meadow voles have small eyes and ears and are active during the daytime. They make trails and runways in grass and sedges, and store seeds and grains as food for winter.

Rock Vole
Microtus chrotorrhinus

Common locally on forested talus slopes, rock voles are not found on mainland Nova Scotia. They have noses that are orange to reddish in colour.

Southern Bog Lemming
Synaptomys cooperi

Common, but found only in a few locations. Found near forested rocky talus slopes.

Woodland Jumping Mouse
Zapus insignis

Common in hardwood and mixed forests. It prefers areas with streams. They hibernate all winter and they don't show their faces until late spring. Its tail has a white tip.

Meadow Jumping Mouse
Zapus hudsonius

Common locally in wet fields, meadows and flood plains. It also hibernates for long periods during fall, winter, and spring. Its tail is not white tipped.

Muskrat *Ondatra Zibethicus*	Common near waterways with muddy banks or cattail marshes. They have a very high reproduction rate, producing several litters per year. Thought to be our bravest mammal, they will stand their ground, even against man.
Norway Rat *Rattus norvegicus*	Introduced and uncommon, the Norway rat appears in urban areas and farmlands.
Black Rat *Rattus ritz*	Introduced through seaports, the black rat has been reported in Chéticamp. It is thought that this rat will not become permanently established here.
Eastern Chipmunk *Tamias striatus*	During some years the chipmunks appear common while other years they seem scarce. Usually they are seen in rocky areas with hardwood trees. They spend the winter in deep hibernation.
American Red Squirrel *Tamiasciurus hudsonicus*	Common in most forested areas, squirrels are active year round gathering and eating nuts. They also eat any animal that is small enough or helpless enough to catch. Squirrels seem to be more commonly found in softwood areas.
Northern Flying Squirrel *Glaucomys sabrinus*	Common in most forest habitats, our one flying squirrel is active only at night. It is rarely seen and uses

woodpecker holes found in trees to sleep in. They climb to the top of spruce trees and drop spruce cones down to be gathered later.

American Beaver
Castor canadensis

Commonly found in rivers and lakes, but rarer up on the highlands. The beaver was trapped to the point of extirpation on the Island, but was reintroduced after World War II. Often criticised for damaging trees, they never clear-cut entire forests like some humans.

Snowshoe/Varying Hare
Lepus americanus

Common in softwood stands. Population fluctuates from year to year. This is the hare that changes its coat from winter white to summer brown.

Ermine (weasel)
Mustela erminea

The smallest of our weasels, it changes colour from winter white to summer brown. It is common in our area and is very curious by nature. Look for them around brush piles and rocky places.

American Marten
Martes americana

A rare animal once common throughout Nova Scotia. Trapping has reduced the marten to only a few individuals hiding in the protection of CapeBreton Highlands National Park. This member of the weasel family prefers living in the mature evergreen forest.

American Mink
Mustela vison

Commonly found near fresh or salt water. They are about the size of a house cat, dark brown with a white patch on their throat.

River Otter
Lontra canadensis

They are common at the mouths of most rivers. Otters can be seen playing their sliding games, even in the summer, on steep shorelines. Our largest member of the weasel family, and the best swimmer and catcher of fish.

Raccoon
Procyon lotor

As a result of the construction of the Canso Causeway in 1956, which connects Cape Breton to the mainland, the raccoon has gained access to the Island. They are found in low numbers around the Cabot Trail.

Red Fox
Vulpes vulpes

Our common fox of fields and headlands. Seen in most open areas from sea level to highland barrens.

Arctic Fox
Alopex lagopus

Rare vagrants, they have been recorded several times, coming here on ice-floes from the far north.

Coyote
Canis latrans

It is thought that when Europeans first came to North America the coyote lived only on the western side of the Mississippi River. Because of our ploughs, fires and forest practices, we have enabled the coyote to migrate all the way to Cape Breton Island. They arrived on the Cabot Trail during the early 1980s.

Timber Wolf *Canis lupus*	Disappeared due to pressure from man during the 1870s. Now absent from all of Nova Scotia.
Bobcat *Lynx rufus*	The bobcat is smaller than the lynx, but a lot more aggressive as a hunter. It stays more or less in the lower elevations. Because it has a more varied diet than the lynx, it is a better competitor during severe winters and therefore has a better survival rate.
Canada Lynx *Lynx lynx*	The lynx is becoming rarer because of pressures from the new arrival of bobcats and coyotes. Restricted to the highland wilderness areas.
Eastern Cougar *Felis concolor*	This endangered cat, our biggest, is thought to live in the wilderness of Cape Breton. Many people have seen this long tailed, tan coloured cat, but no one has taken a photo and there is no physical evidence of its presence.
Western Cougar *Felis concolor missoulensis*	It is known that pet Western cougars have been released in Nova Scotia, and one skull was even found in the woods. It's possible that some, if not most, of our big cat sightings are of this introduced western race.
White-tailed Deer *Odocoileus virginianus*	Introduced to Cape Breton Island in the early part of this century, they are common throughout the lowlands, but are rare on the highlands. They seem to prefer living

in and around disturbed areas created by humans.

Woodland Caribou
Rangifer tarandus

Extirpated. The last caribou was shot in 1925. In the 1960s attempts to reintroduce them in the highlands failed. It appears we have changed the vegetation and landscape to the point that this highly migratory animal cannot exist on Cape Breton Island today.

Moose
Alces alces

Common throughout, moose seem to prefer the higher elevations. The original moose population was hunted to extirpation. They were later reintroduced from a population found in Alberta. Currently their population is large. This is due to the recent spruce budworm damage to highland trees which allowed young shrubs to grow, providing a large source of food for the moose.

American Black Bear
Ursus americanus

Our only bear, it spends its winters in deep sleep under logs and other protected areas. They are sometimes seen on hillsides eating berries during spring and summer. Black bears are common here, but in low numbers.

Human Being
Homo sapiens

Mostly found around the Cabot Trail, they build enclosed nesting areas. They require large amounts of energy to heat their nests and bring food from far away. Active day or night, some degrade their surrounding environment, while others create music – a most complex social mammal.

Harbour Seal
Phoca vitulina

Commonly seen in all coastal waters. Some are thought to migrate to U.S. coastal areas during winter. Easily distinguished from the gray seal by its smaller head and body. They pup in late May to early June on rocky shores and sandbars.

Gray Seal
Halichoerus grypus

The largest seal of our area is found basking in the sunshine on rocks jutting out from Bird Island. Seal pups can be seen in late January and February in the Gulf of St Lawrence. Gray seals have been seen on the highlands in the National Park during winter forays. They do not migrate away from Nova Scotia.

Harp Seal
Phoca groenlandica

Harp seals pup on the ice in March near the Magdalen Islands and appear on our shores until early April. White-coat pups of the harp seal were the mainstay of the sealing industry in the past. They migrate north out of the Gulf of St. Lawrence and are not seen during summer months.

Hooded Seal
Cystophora cristata

Pups are born in late February and March in the same area as the harp seals. Hooded seals migrate after pupping to Greenland and Iceland, and return to pup again the following spring. Very few are ever seen from our shores.

Atlantic Walrus
Odobenus rosmarus

Extirpated. One of the largest herds of Atlantic Walrus in the world once lived between the Magdalen Islands and the western shores of Cape Breton. They were wiped out by Europeans in the late 1700s.

TOOTHED WHALES

Atlantic Harbour Porpoise
Phocaena phocaena

Uncommon, but seen occasionally from whale cruises. Our smallest whale, only 4 to 5 feet in length, makes a loud puffing sound that can be heard far away.

White-sided Dolphin
Lagenorhynchus acutus

Common inshore and offshore, these dolphins leap right out of the water. Very fast swimmers, they are sometimes seen from whale cruises, but are rarely spotted from shore.

Beluga Whale
Delphinapterus leucas

The occasional straggler is left behind as others pass by Bay St. Lawrence. They are a distinctive white colour.

Long-finned Pilot Whale
Globicephola melaena

Very common near the coastline and offshore, the pilot whales follow the short-fin squid and mackerel around the coast. Often seen from whale cruises, they have little visible blow, a large black dorsal fin and often show their tail when diving. Pods of up to 200 whales are seen annually.

Orca (Killer Whale)
Orcinas orca

Uncommon, stays offshore. Some Orcas were stranded on beaches in Prince Edward Island in the 1980s. Rarely seen from whale cruises and there are no recorded shore observations.

Sperm Whale
Physeter macrocephalus

Rare in our waters, the reported sightings include one from a whale cruise and another from French Mountain Look-off. The largest of the toothed whales is thought to hunt the giant squid (up to 50 feet long). The sperm whale's blow is made at a 45° angle, their dorsal fin is not prominent, they have a squarish head and can show their tail when diving.

BALEEN WHALES

Minke Whale
Balaenoptera acutorostrata

Our smallest baleen whale (20 to 30 feet) shows no blow, has a sharply curved small dorsal fin and does not show its tail when diving. Often seen from whale cruises, minkes travel alone rather than in groups.

Humpback Whale
Megaptera novaeangliae

Locally uncommon inshore and offshore. Humpbacks usually summer in waters off Newfoundland, but they sometimes frequent northern Cape Breton waters. Their population seems to be on the rise since the moratorium on commercial whaling in Canada. They are the showiest of the whales. They have a bushy, low blow, show an irregular low dorsal fin, and they sometimes show their tails which can be used to identify individual hump backs.

Atlantic Gray Whale
Eschrichtius robustus

Extinct. Population destroyed by Basque whalers in the 16th century.

Sei Whale
Balaenoptera borealis

Uncommon, this large offshore whale (45 to 60 feet) is rarely seen from shore. It is difficult to tell the difference between sei and fin whales. They are in the same size range and their tall blows are similar.

Fin Whale
Balaenoptera physalus

Common offshore and sometimes inshore, fin whales are seen in late spring and through the summer. The fin whale is large averaging 60 to 70 feet long. When surfacing it shows a tall 20 foot blow, then a medium sized dorsal fin. It rarely shows its tail. They are usually found in small groups and are rarely seen alone.

Blue Whale
Balaenoptera musculus

Uncommon to rare. They spend the summer in the Gulf of St. Lawrence. The blue whale is our largest, up to 100 feet long. Sometimes they float on the surface. Only a very few sightings have been reported in our area. Bay St. Lawrence is probably the best place to look for these great animals as they enter the Gulf.

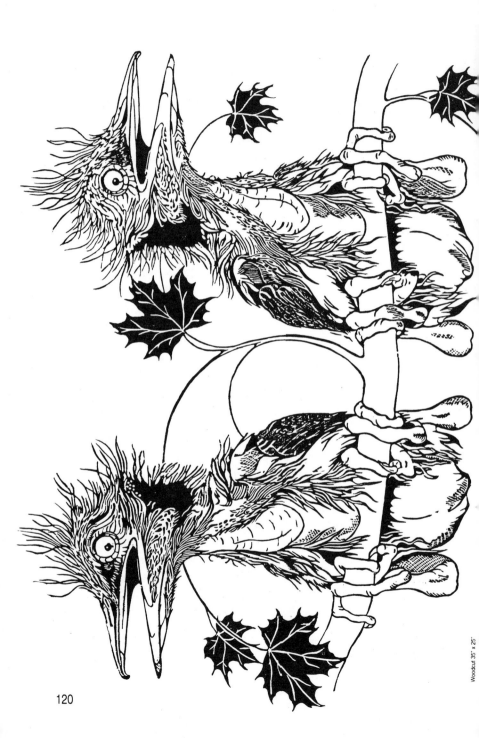

Woodcut 35" x 25"

120

BIRDS OF THE CABOT TRAIL

The oldest bird fossils date back 200 million years. Recall that this was when the Earth started its present orbit around the Milky Way. We will probably never know what types of birds were here then, but we do have a good knowledge of the 234 different species found along the Cabot Trail today.

The following list of birds, their abundance and what habitats they prefer is a product of the observations of many people. Over the last fifty years or more many truly hardworking naturalists have walked through our woods recording the birds. The letters after the birds' names refer to the following information:

Relative Abundance (RA)   Residence Status (RS)

c	common	p	permanent resident
unc	uncommon	sr	summer resident
r	rare	wr	winter resident
vr	very rare, maybe	m	migrating through area
	seen only once a	v	visitor, irregular
	decade	ca	casual
		ac	accidental (storm birds)

Common Name	RA	RS	Preferred Habitat
Red-throated Loon	unc-r	m	coastal waters, spring & fall
Common Loon	c	p	fresh and salt waters
Pied-billed Grebe	r	m	fresh water, flood plains & bays
Horned Grebe	r	m	coastal waters, spring & fall
Red-necked Grebe	unc-r	m	coastal waters, fall & winter
Northern Fulmar	unc	m	Atlantic coastal waters
Greater Shearwater	unc	v	offshore waters, summer
Sooty Shearwater	unc-r	m	offshore waters, summer
Leach's Storm-petrel	unc	sr	nest on St. Paul's Island
Northern Gannet	unc	v-m	summer visitor, spring & fall
Great Cormorant	c	sr	coastal waters & islands

Double-crested Cormorant	c	sr	coastal waters, bays & islands
American Bittern	r	sr	fresh & salt water marshes
Great Blue Heron	c	sr	harbours, bays & marshes
Great Egret	r	v	Englishtown and Baddeck
Little Blue Heron	r	ca	three records to date
Cattle Egret	r	v	Chéticamp two sightings
Glossy Ibis	r	v	Cape North & Chéticamp
Snow Goose	r	ca	coastal waters
Brant	r	ca	coastal waters, fall
Canada Goose	unc	m	coastal waters & interior lakes
Wood Duck	r	sr	St. Ann's Harbour
Green-winged Teal	unc	sr	lakes, bays & marshes
Black Duck	c	p	most water habitats
Mallard	r	v	rivers & lakes
Pintail	r	m	spring & fall
Blue-winged Teal	unc	sr	fertile marshes & estuaries
Northern Shoveller	r	ca	Aspy Bay, few sightings
American Wigeon	r	v	Nyanza Bay, one sighting
Canvasback	r	v	one sighting only
Ring-necked Duck	unc	sr	lakes, ponds, stillwater
Greater Scaup	c	m	coastal waters, fall to spring
Common Eider	unc-c	p	coastal waters, Bird Island
King Eider	r	ca	coastal waters
Harlequin Duck	r	wr	coastal waters, fall to spring
Oldsquaw	c	wr	coastal waters, fall to spring
Black Scoter	r	wr	offshore waters, fall to spring
Surf Scoter	unc	wr	coastal waters, fall to spring
White-winged Scoter	c	p	coastal waters, rare in summer
Common Goldeneye	c-r	p	rare in summer, lakes, ponds
Barrow's Goldeneye	r	wr	coastal waters, fall to spring
Bufflehead	r	wr	coastal waters, fall to spring
Hooded Merganser	r	sr	Warren Lake and Baddeck
Common Merganser	c	p	most rivers and many brooks
Red-breasted Merganser	unc	p	river estuaries, sandbars
Turkey Vulture	r	v	winter, two sightings

Relative Abundance (RA)		Residence Status (RS)	
c	common	p	permanent resident
unc	uncommon	sr	summer resident
r	rare	wr	winter resident
vr	very rare, maybe	m	migrating through area
	seen only once a	v	visitor, irregular
	decade	ca	casual
		ac	accidental (storm birds)

Osprey	unc-r	sr	river estuaries, lakes, bays
Bald Eagle	c	p	Bras d'Or Lake, rivers, coastline
Northern Harrier	unc	sr	beaches, farms, bogs, meadows
Sharp-shinned Hawk	unc	sr	evergreen and mixed forest
Broad-winged Hawk	r	ca	hardwood forest
Northern Goshawk	r	p	mature mixed forest
Red-tailed Hawk	unc	sr	barrens, open spaces, farms
Rough-legged Hawk	r	wr	headland & highland plateau
Golden Eagle	r	sr	remote highlands and cliffs
American Kestrel	unc	sr	farmlands, clear-cuts
Merlin	unc	sr	forest edges, beaches, dunes
Peregrine Falcon	r	m	highlands
Gyrfalcon	r	wv	few sightings
Ring-necked Pheasant	r	p	Chéticamp area
Spruce Grouse	unc	p	highland plateau
Ruffed Grouse	c	p	mixed forest, old orchards
Virginia Rail	r	v	one record
Sora	r	sr	fresh & brackish marshes
Purple Gallinule	r	ac	one record
American Coot	r	ac	one record
Black-bellied Plover	unc-c	m	beaches, marshes, fall
Lesser Golden Plover	r	m	fields, beaches, marshes, fall
Semipalmated Plover	unc-c	m	mudflats, marshes, beaches
Piping Plover	r	v	Dingwall Beach
Killdeer	r	sr	open lands along the coast
Greater Yellowlegs	unc	sr	bogs & barrens, plateau
Lesser Yellowlegs	unc	m	July to October, beaches
Solitary Sandpiper	r	m	shallow wet areas
Willet	r-unc	sr	Aspy Bay, Chéticamp area
Spotted Sandpiper	c	sr	most rivers and lakeshores
Whimbrel	r	m	beaches, headlands, White Point
Hudsonian Godwit	r	m	Bird Islands, headlands
Ruddy Turnstone	r	m	rocky shoreline, fall
Red Knot	unc	m	coastal areas, spring & fall
Sanderling	unc	m	sandy beaches & mudflats
Semipalmated Sandpiper	unc-c	m	sandy beaches & mudflats
Western Sandpiper	r	m	sandy beaches & mudflats
Least Sandpiper	unc	m	sandy beaches & mudflats
White-rumped Sandpiper	unc-c	m	mudflats near salty marshes
Pectoral Sandpiper	r	m	beaches,
Purple Sandpiper	r	wr	near surf on rocky coastline
Stilt Sandpiper	r	ca	grassy marshes
Buff-breasted Sandpiper	r	v	Ingonish, one sighting only

Short-billed Dowitcher	unc	m	low tide mudflats & marshes
Common Snipe	unc	sr	shallow marshes and bogs
American Woodcock	unc	sr	wet hardwood forest & swamps
Red-necked Phalarope	r-unc	m	Dingwall area, Aspy Bay
Red Phalarope	r-unc	m	Cape North & Cape St Lawrence
Black-headed Gull	r	wr	coastal areas
Bonaparte's Gull	r	m	coastal bays and river estuaries
Ring-billed Gull	r	v	coastal and freshwater areas
Herring Gull	c	p	coastal and freshwater areas
Iceland Gull	c	wr	coastal waters
Glaucous Gull	c	wr	coastal waters
Great Black-backed Gull	c	p	coastal areas
Black-legged Kittiwake	unc-r	sr	nest on Bird Islands, offshore
Caspian Tern	unc-r	v	bays near headlands
Common Tern	unc	sr	seen diving in coastal waters
Arctic Tern	r	sr	fresh or salt waters
Dovekie	unc-r	wr	Atlantic coastal waters
Common Murre	r	ca	coastal waters
Thick-billed Murre	r	v	only a few sightings
Razorbill	r	sr	nest on Bird Island, offshore
Black Guillemot	c	p	coastal areas with cliffs
Atlantic Puffin	unc	sr	nest on Bird Islands
Rock Dove	r	p	villages, farms
Mourning Dove	unc-r	sr	open pine forest, farms
Black-billed Cuckoo	r	v	open woodlands, forest edges
Yellow-billed Cuckoo	r	ac	few sightings
Great Horned Owl	unc	p	hardwood and softwood forest
Snowy Owl	r-unc	wr	headlands, fields
Barred Owl	unc	p	mixed woodlands & hardwoods
Long-eared Owl	r	sr	woodlands large or small
Short-eared Owl	r	wr	marshes, coastal bogs,grassland
Boreal Owl	r	p	forested northern bogs
Northern Saw-whet Owl	unc	p	highlands or lowlands forested
Common Nighthawk	unc	sr	clear-cuts and meadows
Chimney Swift	unc-r	sr	open areas near older trees

Relative Abundance (RA)

c	*common*
unc	*uncommon*
r	*rare*
vr	*very rare, maybe*
	seen only once a
	decade

Residence Status (RS)

p	*permanent resident*
sr	*summer resident*
wr	*winter resident*
m	*migrating through area*
v	*visitor, irregular*
ca	*casual*
ac	*accidental (storm birds)*

Ruby-throated Hummingbird	unc	sr	open woods, gardens, orchards
Belted Kingfisher	c	sr	rivers, lakes, saltwater bays
Red-headed Woodpecker	r	ac	one winter sighting
Yellow-bellied Sapsucker	unc-r	sr	hardwoods, birches & poplars
Downy Woodpecker	c-unc	sr	orchards, woodlands, parks
Hairy Woodpecker	unc	sr	open woodlands
Three-toed Woodpecker	r	p	highlands boreal forest
Black-backed Woodpecker	unc-r	p	conifer forest, jack pine stands
Northern Flicker	c	sr	clearings, roadsides, with trees
Pileated Woodpecker	unc	p	mature forest, big trees
Olive-sided Flycatcher	unc	sr	disturbed forest, clear-cuts
Eastern Wood Peewee	unc	sr	prefers hardwoods near stream
Yellow-bellied Flycatcher	c	sr	conifer and coastal forest
Alder Flycatcher	unc	sr	stream edges, alders & willows
Least Flycatcher	c-unc	sr	mostly found in hardwoods
Eastern Phoebe	r	sr	near streams, under bridges
Say's Phoebe	r	ac	one fall sighting
Eastern Kingbird	r	sr	found in open areas
Horned Lark	unc	wr	coastal beaches & headlands
Tree Swallow	c	sr	all rivers, most lakes edges
Bank Swallow	c	sr	coastal cliffs & river banks
Cliff Swallow	r	sr	nest on bridges and buildings
Barn Swallow	unc	sr	near buildings and farms
Gray Jay	unc	p	higher elevations, forested
Blue Jay	c-unc	p	lower elevations, near humans
Common Crow	c	p	disturbed lands, settlements
Common Raven	c	p	wilderness areas, coastline
Black-capped Chickadee	c	p	mixed woodlands of lowlands
Boreal Chickadee	c-unc	p	conifer forest of plateau
Red-breasted Nuthatch	unc-c	p	softwoods of highlands & coast
White-breasted Nuthatch	r	sr	Ingonish area, hardwoods
Brown Creeper	r	p	mixed woodlands, tree trunks
Winter Wren	unc	sr	upper river valleys with brush
Golden-crowned Kinglet	c	p	found in evergreen woodlands
Ruby-crowned Kinglet	c	sr	conifer or mixed woodlands
Eastern Bluebird	r	v	Chéticamp area, very rare
Veery	r	sr	mixed forest, Chéticamp River
Gray-cheeked Thrush (bicknelli)	r	sr	conifer forest close to barrens
Swainson's Thrush	c	sr	almost all wooded areas
Hermit Thrush	c-unc	sr	mixed woods with openings
American Robin	c	sr	frequents open areas & woods
Gray Catbird	r	sr	near settlements
Northern Mockingbird	r	v	around in winter

Brown Thrasher	r	ca	spring or fall
Water Pipit	unc	m	coastal beaches & headlands
Bohemian Waxwing	r	ca	occasionally during winter
Cedar Waxwing	unc	sr	open woodlands, road edges
Northern Shrike	r	ca	winter visitor
Loggerhead Shrike	r	sr	one nest recorded only
European Starling	c-unc	p	occurs in settled areas
Solitary Vireo	unc	sr	open mixed woodlands
Warbling Vireo	r	sr	hardwoods, in Margaree Valley
Philadelphia Vireo	r	sr	nest in Aspy Bay, hardwoods
Red-eyed Vireo	c	sr	mixed and deciduous woodlands
Tennessee Warbler	c-unc	sr	conifer forest with poor drainage
Nashville Warbler	unc-r	sr	openings in dense mixed forest
Northern Parula Warbler	c	sr	mixed mature woodlands
Yellow Warbler	unc	sr	distured habitats in wet areas
Chestnut-sided Warbler	r	sr	nest near Bay St. Lawrence
Magnolia Warbler	c	sr	evergreen and mixed woodlands
Cape May Warbler	unc-r	sr	mature coastal conifer forest
Black-throated Blue Warbler	r	m	hardwoods, valleys & lowlands
Yellow-rumped Warbler	c	sr	widespread in mixed forest
Black-throated Green Warbler	unc-r	sr	mature conifer forest
Blackburnian Warbler	c	sr	widespread in mixed forest
Pine Warbler	r	ac	winter sightings only
Palm Warbler	r	sr	nest in Lowland Cove area
Bay-breasted Warbler	unc	sr	nest only in conifer trees
Blackpoll Warbler	c-unc	sr	areas with stunted spruce trees
Black-and-white Warbler	c-unc	sr	mixed woods along rivers
American Redstart	c	sr	deciduous woodlands
Ovenbird	c-unc	sr	hardwood valleys & mixed wood
Northern Waterthrush	unc	sr	alders near rivers, lakes, bogs
Mourning Warbler	c	sr	shrubs, bushes, clear-cuts
Common Yellowthroat	c	sr	areas with thickets & shrubs
Wilson's Warbler	r	sr	shrublands & early forest
Canada Warbler	r	sr	nest in Bay St. Lawrence area
Scarlet Tanager	r	v	spring visitors
Rose-breasted Grosbeak	unc	sr	deciduous woodland near water
Indigo Bunting	r	ac	few sightings
Painted Bunting	r	ca	pair sighted, Red R. area, spring
Dickcissel	r	ca	fall, Ingonish
Rufous-sided Towhee	r	ac	winter, few sightings
American Tree Sparrow	r	v	fall or winter
Chipping Sparrow	c-unc	sr	open woods at lower elevations
Vesper Sparrow	r	sr	short grass pasture, Margaree

Savannah Sparrow	unc-r	sr	grassy meadows, dry marshes
Sharp-tailed Sparrow	r	sr	salt marshes and dunes
Fox Sparrow	unc	sr	most scrub woodlands
Song Sparrow	c-unc	sr	bushy areas, edges of woods
Lincoln's Sparrow	c-unc	sr	bogs and alder swales
Swamp Sparrow	c-unc	sr	wet areas with shrub & grasses
White-throated Sparrow	c	sr	open areas, meadows, clearings
White-crowned Sparrow	r	m	open woodlands, spring, fall
Dark-eyed Junco	c	p	throughout, from beach to bog
Snow Bunting	unc-r	wr	fields and meadows, headlands
Bobolink	unc-r	sr	farmlands, fields
Red-winged Blackbird	c	sr	marshes, rivers, wet meadows
Yellow-headed Blackbird	r	v	one sighting only
Rusty Blackbird	unc	sr	spruce bogs, damp alder swales
Common Grackle	c-unc	sr	open woodlands with meadows
Brown-headed Cowbird	unc-r	sr	old fields and farmlands
Northern Oriole	unc	v	urban gardens
Pine Grosbeak	unc	p	conifer and mixed forest
Purple Finch	c	p	throughout our area
Red Crossbill	r	p	conifer woods, hillsides
White-winged Crossbill	unc-r	p	conifer woods
Common Redpoll	c-unc	wr	open areas with shrubs
Pine Siskin	c-unc	p	conifer forest
American Goldfinch	c	sr	open woodland, meadows, fields
Evening Grosbeak	c-unc	p	open mixed woodlands
House Sparrow	unc	p	around settlement

Relative Abundance (RA)		*Residence Status (RS)*	
c	*common*	*p*	*permanent resident*
unc	*uncommon*	*sr*	*summer resident*
r	*rare*	*wr*	*winter resident*
vr	*very rare, maybe*	*m*	*migrating through area*
	seen only once a	*v*	*visitor, irregular*
	decade	*ca*	*casual*
		ac	*accidental (storm birds)*

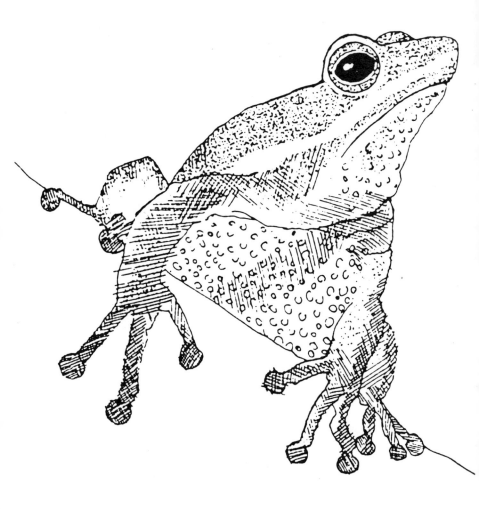

AMPHIBIANS

TOADS & FROGS	HABITAT	COMMENTS
Eastern American Toad	Most terrestrial areas; found in ponds, lakes and streams when breeding in spring	-breeds in early spring -terrestrial -eats insects, beetles, worms and ants -hibernates in burrows in forest soil
Green Frog	Practically any fresh-water, wet meadows and grassy woodlands	-breeds in early summer; mostly aquatic -distinctive banjo string-like call -makes a startled noise if frightened -calls freely during day or night
Mink Frog	Vegetated shallows of lakes and slow moving streams	-our last frog to breed in summer -mostly aquatic in nature -gives off musky odour when frightened -easily confused with green frogs
Northern Leopard Frog	Meadows, old fields, grassy woodlands near aquatic breeding sites	-breeds in late spring (May); terrestrial -eats grasshoppers and other insects -a good jumper -call sounds like a "snore" -hibernates in pond mud -characteristic of most of Canada
Northern Spring Peeper	Inhabits woodlands near ponds, quiet streams, lakes, and coves	-one of the first frogs to breed in spring -gathers in great numbers while mating -terrestrial; has special adaptations on toes for climbing trees and bushes -hibernates under leaf litter -well camouflaged; our smallest frog
Pickerel Frog	Lakeshores, bogs, meadows, streams, and grassy fields	-breeds in late spring (May) -aquatic and terrestrial -few snakes will eat it because its skin gland secretions are distasteful -call is a low snore -calls while submerged
Wood Frog	Moist wooded areas; migrates to ponds, bogs	-one of the first frogs to breed in spring -terrestrial

and ditches to breed

-large numbers at breeding ponds
-not often found after breeding
-call is a low pitched clacking or
  like a duck quacking in the distance
-has facial mask like the Lone Ranger
-characteristic of Canada, coast to coast

SALAMANDERS	HABITAT	COMMENTS
Blue-spotted Salamander	Woodlands near ponds and slow, vegetated streams & alder swamps. Found under rocks and rotten logs	-breeds in early spring -adults are terrestrial -larvae are aquatic -restricted to areas with gypsum
Eastern Redback Salamander	Inhabits most woodlands but can be found in non-wooded areas with blueberries	-breeds in autumn and lays eggs the following June; no aquatic stage -lays eggs in rotten logs -eats insects, earthworms and beetles -hides under logs, rocks, etc. -eggs are guarded by adults
Four-toed Salamander	Deciduous or mixed woodland near sphagnum bogs or boggy streams that are used for egg laying	-breeds in fall and lays eggs in the spring -known to share nesting sites -four toes on front and back feet -rare & endangerd in Nova Scotia -vulnerable to human disturbance when nesting
Red-spotted Newt	Larvae and adults live in ponds, slow moving streams and lakes. Juveniles (red efts) live in woodland, on or under leaves	-breeds in early spring -three distinct appearances: larvae, juveniles, adults -eats insects, leeches, worms, frog eggs -few predators eat newts -skin glands produce an untasty substance
Yellow-spotted Salamander	Woodlands near bogs, ponds, lakes, coves and boggy streams. Adults live underground.	-breeds in early spring and often in great numbers -adults are terrestrial -larvae are aquatic -hard to find after breeding

REPTILES

SNAKES	*HABITAT*	*COMMENTS*
Eastern Smooth Green Snake	Grassy sites along ponds, lakeshores, streams, as well as old fields and roadsides	-lays eggs under or in rotten logs and forest litter
Maritime Garter Snake	Rocky woodlands, fields, swamps, bogs, and roadsides	-live young -first to appear in spring -hibernates in large numbers
Northern Redbelly Snake	Under rocks and logs in both moist and dry sites	-smallest reptile in Cape Breton -nocturnal -live young
Northern Ringneck Snake	Hardwoods and mixed woods usually adjacent to ponds, lakes and streams	-lays eggs under rocks and logs -nocturnal and rarely seen -can be confused with Redbelly Snakes

TURTLES	*HABITAT*	*COMMENTS*
Atlantic Leatherback Sea Turtle	Warm waters of the Gulf Stream	-occasionally seen from May to Sept -most of its life spent at sea -largest living turtle -an endangered species
Common Snapping Turtle	Large ponds, streams and lakes, near sand or fine gravel used for nesting	-short tempered -rarely found basking -a few introduced to the Cabot Trail
Wood Turtle	Slow moving streams with sand or gravel for nesting. Not often found on the Cabot Trail. Trail	-wanders extensively on land -eats plants, worms, snails -only naturally occuring turtle found in Cape Breton

ARTHROPODS
Spiders, Pseudoscorpions, Ticks, Mites, Insects, Butterflies and Moths

A considerable amount of time has been spent attempting to understand the arthropod fauna of Cape Breton Highlands National Park. Arthropods are animals that do not have a backbone. Their bodies are in segments and their legs are hard on the surface and are used as an exoskeleton. The lists accompanying the following text on insects were compiled from a study done by J.D. Lafontaine et. al. of the Biosystematics Research Centre published in 1987.

Over several years thirty six different scientists studied the northern Cape Breton area. It is thought that over 10,000 different arthropod species live here and, because they are so numerous, we cannot list every species. Instead, we will focus on the bigger, showy types like butterflies and moths. Spiders, my favourite arthropods, will be discussed as well as ticks and mites. Below is a chart which attempts to summarize the different types and the number of species of these animals found along the peaceful Cabot Trail.

Spiders

Let's start with spiders. I like spiders a lot and maybe you will grow to like them too. Spiders are distinguished from other arthropods by their fang–like mouth parts and because they have no antennae. Pseudoscorpions, mites, ticks and spiders all have these characteristics in common. But spiders are the only ones that also produce silk from their abdomen. They are also distinguished by their four pairs of legs, unlike insects which have only three pairs.

It is thought that at least 300 different species of spiders live in our area. To date, 233 species of spiders have been reported. The commonly found ones in Cape Breton include the following:

Agelenidae	Funnel-web Spider	Philodromidae	Crab Spider
Araneidae	Orb Spider	Salticidae	Jumping Spider
Clubionidae	Sac Spider	Tetragnathidae	Orb Spider
Graphosidae	Ground Spider	Theridiidae	Cobweb Spider
Hahiidae	Spider	Theridiosmatidae	Orb Spiders
Lycosidae	Wolf Spider	Thomisidae	Crab Spider

Pseudoscorpions

Four species of pseudoscorpions were found in our area, often in bog mosses, and in rotting logs and leaf litter in mixed forests. The most common was Chelifer cancroides; it was just about everywhere, especially in books and on insects like flies and beetles. The other three were restricted to the more natural environments. Another six are thought to live around the Cabot Trail, but have eluded the prying eye of humans.

Chelifer cancroides	Microbisium confusum
Microbisium brunneum	Pseudogarupus banksi

Ticks

Scientists anticipate finding approximately ten species of ticks in Cape Breton, but to date only three species have been found. American dog ticks, although common in southwestern Nova Scotia, have not been found to have a viable population on Cape Breton. The ticks known to be in Cape Breton are listed below.

Rabbit Tick
Haemaphysalis leporispalustris
– found on birds, rabbits, mice, and rarely on humans

Brown Dog Tick
Rhipicephalus saguineus
- found on dogs, coyotes, rabbits, deer, and occasionally humans

Marine Bird Tick
Ixodes uriae
– found on auks, murres, puffins, and cormorants

Mites

Five hundred and twenty nine species of mites have been found near the Cabot Trail, but researchers expect to find approximately 1600 different types in total. Mites are tiny in size. They eat almost everything from pollen to fungi, and you'll find them nesting on birds,insects, mammals and other mites. Soil mites are essential animals in the recycling of nutrients and the decomposition of leaf litter. To give you an idea of the many different types of mites thought to be in northern Cape Breton, a short and very incomplete list follows:

Actinedid mites	Gustavioid mites
Ameroseiid mites	Oribatid mites
Ascid mites	Phytophagous mites
Bamasid mites	Psoroptoid mites
Errophyoid mites	Whirligig mites

Other Arthropods

Also found in our area are three strange arthropod-like creatures that don't fit into the previous groups and are not thought to be insects. They are usually located in damp places; under leaves, in moss, under stones and in rotting logs. They are the millipedes, centipedes and the myriapods.

INSECTS

The many different types of insects found around the Cabot Trail often do not have common names. The class names of the insects are listed on page 138, but to give you an idea of the diversity, here are some of the common names of insects you might find in our area:

ambush bugs	crickets	katydids	scorpion flies
ants	damsel bugs	lace wings	silver fish
assassin bugs	damselflies	lace flies	skippers
back swimmers	deer flies	ladybird beetles	snowfleas
bedbugs	dobson flies	leaf hoppers	soldier bugs
bee flies	dragonflies	leaf miners	spittlebugs
bees	dusty wings	locusts	springtails
beetles	earwigs	longhorned beetles	squash bugs
black flies	fish flies	maggots	stilt bugs
blowflies	flat bugs	mayflies	stink bugs
booklice	flower flies	midges	stoneflies
bristletails	fruit flies	mourning cloaks	sucking lice
bumble bees	giant waterbugs	mosquitoes	tree hoppers
butterflies	glowworms	moths	true bugs
caddis flies	gnats	no-see-ums	wasps
carrion beetles	grasshoppers	plant bugs	water striders
chewing lice	ground beetles	plant hoppers	water boatman
chinch bugs	honey bees	predaceous	weevils
click beetles	horse flies	diving beetles	whirligig beetles
cockroaches	house flies	robber flies	wood nymphs
crane flies	june beetles	scarab beetles	yellow jackets

BUTTERFLIES and MOTHS

Butterflies and moths are very important creatures in the intricate web of life on Cape Breton Island. Some pollinate flowers, thus enhancing plant life, while others, such as the spruce budworm, kill trees. Birds and bats would have difficulty feeding their young without this group of animals. The butterflies of Cape Breton Highlands National Park are classified into six families. The census on the following page summarizes the number of species known and expected to occur in Northern Cape Breton.

Census of Cape Breton Highlands National Park Lepidoptera

Superfamily	Common Name	Estimated No. of species	Species recorded
Bomgycoidea	Giant silkworm moths	7	3
Copromorphoidea	Small moths	5	1
Cossoidea	Leaf-roller moths	3	0
Eriocranioidea	Small moths	1	0
Gelechioidea	Small moths	100	5
Geometroidea	Inch worms	154	76
Hepialoidea	Small moths	2	0
Hesperioidea	Butterflies	10	9
Incurvarioidea	Small moths	2	0
Micropterigoidea	Small moths	1	0
Nepticuloidea	Small moths	20	0
Noctuoidea	Owlet moths	372	196
Papilionoidea	Butterflies	38	26
Pterophoroidea	Plum moths	12	1
Pyraloidea	Leaf-rollers	75	22
Sesioidea	Clear wing moths	5	0
Sphingoidea	Hawk moths	14	7
Tineoidea	Small moths	50	1
Tortricoidea	Bud worms	150	50
Yponomeutoidea	Small moths	20	4
Zygaenoidea	Slug caterpillar moths	3	0
Total		**1044**	**401**

*Butterflies of Northern Cape Breton
are classified in six families:*

Hesperiidae
Skippers
Arctic Skipper
Dreamy dusky wings
European Skipper
Hobomok Skipper
Least Skipper
Long Dash
Peck's Skipper
Tawny Edged Skipper

Lycanidae
Gossamer–winged
American Copper
Bog Copper
Brown Elfin
Crowberry Blue
Silvery Blue
Spring Azure

Papillionidae
Swallowtails
Black Swallowtails
Short Tailed Swallowtails
Tiger Swallowtails

Satyridae
Satyrs and Wood Nymphs
Jutta Arctic
Wood Nymphs

Nymphalidae
Brush–footed Butterflies
American Painted Lady
Aphrodite Fritillary
Atlantis Fritillary
Great Spangled Fritillary
Green Comma
Mourning Cloak
Painted Lady
Pearl Crescent
Purple Lesser Fritillary
Red Admiral
Silver Bordered Fritillary
White Admiral

Pieridae
Whites and Sulphurs
Common Sulphur
European Cabbage Butterflies
Pink Edged Sulphur

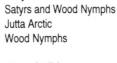

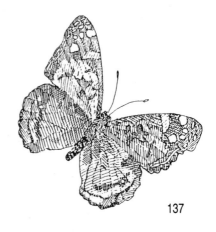

Census of the Insects and Arachnids
of Cape Breton Highlands National Park

Class / Order	Common Name	Estimated No. of species in Park	No.of species recorded in Park
Araneae	Spiders	300	233
Opiliones	Harvestmen	4	0
Pseudoscorpionida	Pseudoscorpions	10	4
Parasitiformes	Ticks and Mites	225	70
Acariformes	Mites	1600	462
Diplopada	Millipedes	30	3
Chilopoda	Centipedes	?	2
Symphyla	Myriapods	1	0
Collembola	Spring tails, Snow fleas	200	?
Microcoryphia	Jumping Springtails	?	0
Thysanura	Silverfish	?	0
Ephemeroptera	May flies	50	40
Odonata	Dragon & Damsel Flies	40	37
Plecoptera	Stoneflies	35	32
Dictuoptera	Cockroach	2	0
Dermaptera	Earwigs	2	1
Gryllopterra	Grasshoppers	8	7
Orthopterra	Crickets	14	10
Psocoptera	Book Lice	25	0
Mallophaga	Chewing Lice	?	0
Anoplura	Sucking Lice	20	?
Homoptera	Leaf hoppers	214	161
Hemiptera	True Bugs	320	100
Thysanoptera	Thrips	15	8
Megaloptera	Dobson flies	2	1
Neuroptera	Laceflies	20	4
Coleoptera	Beetles	1349	770
Mecoptera	Scorpion flies	5	2
Diptera	True Flies	1900	715
Siphonaptera	Flies	30	0
Lepidoptera	Butterflies & Moths	1044	401
Trichoptera	Caddisflies	50	2
Hymenoptera	Ants, Wasp, & Bees	2850	985
	TOTAL	**11280**	**4072**

FISH

Fishing is a popular sport in Cape Breton, and visitors often want to know what kinds of fish people catch. Some fish are only found far out to sea. Many others are found near the shore and the following list is of the inshore fish which, for the most part, live in saltwater.

American cod	American smelt	Atlantic catfish	Atlantic halibut
Atlantic mackerel	Atlantic silverside	Bluefin tuna	Capelin
Cusk	Greenland halibut	Haddock	Herring
Lumpfish	Monkfish	Pollock	Redfish
Red hake	Spiny dogfish	Swordfish	Winter flounder

Other fish can be found in both salt and freshwater, like the American eel, rainbow smelt, Atlantic salmon, gaspereau, brown trout, *speckled trout and *rainbow trout (*introduced species). If you plan on fishing in Cape Breton you will need a fishing license and you must be familiar with Nova Scotia's fishing regulations. If you plan on fishing in the National Park you will also need a National Park fishing license. If fishing for salmon you will need a tag and you must use a tied fly.

OTHER ANIMALS

There are many animals that are so small and hidden that you probably will not see them. They are responsible for our soil's productivity. The list of these small animals is very long and composed mainly of Latin names, so we won't include them here. It includes organisms like bacteria, protozoans, nematodes and worms. The large worms, the kind we use for fishing, are called earthworms. They have a band around their middle and all seventeen species were introduced after the arrival of the Europeans to Nova Scotia. They also introduced several snails, although some are native to the Island. Six of the nine slug species found in Nova Scotia were also introduced.

VEGETATION OF NORTHERN CAPE BRETON

Plants in Cape Breton grow everywhere, from sea level with its salt spray to the tundra-like highest elevations in Nova Scotia. They have had to adapt to drastic changes, from living on the equator to periodic glaciation. Most of the plants were in Cape Breton before mankind came into existence.

Over 1,661 plants have been found to date in northern Cape Breton. Rare relics of the cold past grow on north facing, damp ledges near high waterfalls. Arctic willows, bilberries and dwarf birches of the far north are found on the highland barrens. Acadian Hardwood Forests of sugar maple, white pine, ash, hemlock, red oak, beech and elm are now found in undisturbed valleys and hillsides. Northern Boreal Forest of balsam fir and white birch are on the highest elevations, over 1000 feet (300 m). Bogs and northern wet forests of black spruce and tamarack are found where drainage is poor. The Coastal Forest is white spruce and white birch. Beaches and dunes, estuaries and marshes, rocky barrens and headlands; all these diverse conditions on one island make Cape Breton a botanist's paradise.

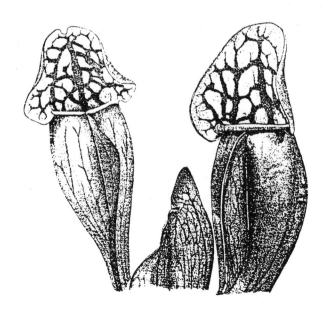

FORESTS OF NORTHERN CAPE BRETON

A forest is composed of many things; thousands of different species of life, from small insects to large old trees. But because we usually think of a forest as just trees, we'll limit the discussion in this section to these particular types of plants.

Cape Breton is in the Acadian Forest Region, a region on the border of the cold far north and warmer southern forest. As a result, you'll find both forest types under the right conditions. Southern trees are sugar maple, elm, red oak, white and black ash, ironwood, white pine, beech, yellow birch and hemlock. Northern trees are aspen, poplar, white birch, red maple, white spruce and fir.

Hardwood is another expression for broad leaf trees and softwood refers to needle bearing trees like pine, spruce, fir and tamarack. It doesn't strictly mean the wood itself is hard or soft. Deciduous is another name for broad leaf trees, because they usually lose their leaves in the winter. Conifer means not losing all the leaves annually, and usually all conifers have needle-like leaves. Tamarack is our one exception; it loses its leaves each winter.

These broad terms don't explain the differences in our trees, nor do they separate our trees into only two groups, but they help. There are still the introduced trees like apple, white poplar and English oak, and in the wet places, tamarack and black spruce. Most of the southern trees do not make it to Newfoundland only 45 km to the north.

WILDFLOWER BLOOM SEQUENCE

The following list of wildflowers was compiled in 1984 for Cape Breton Highlands National Park. I found that the wildflowers tended to bloom two weeks earlier on the western side of the Island compared to the eastern side. When I compiled this list I was hoping it would help me remember when each flower blooms so I could write about them in winter. It did help, and I hope it helps you. These are the flowers most people see but the list is not exhaustive.

Common Name	Latin Name	Location	Bloom Date
Mayflower	Epigaea repens	Franey Trail	May 13
Coltsfoot	Tussilago farfara	Franey Trail	May 13
Red Maple	Acer rubrum	Ingonish Beach	May 13
Pussy Willow	Salix discolor	Ingonish Beach	May 13
Potentilla sp.		Ingonish Beach	May 13
Dutchman's Breeches	Dicentra cucullaria	Lone Shieling Trail	May 15
Rose Twisted Stalk	Streptopus roseus	Lone Shieling Trail	May 15
Spring Beauty	Claytonia caroliniana	Lone Shieling Trail	May 15
Strawberry	Fragaria virginia	Chéticamp	May 15
Marsh Marigold	Caltha palustris	Chéticamp	May 15
Leatherleaf	Chamaedaphne calyculata	French Mtn. Bog Trail	May 15
Sweet gale	Myrica gale	French Mtn. Bog Trail	May 15
Dandelion	Taraxacum officinale	French Mtn. Bog Trail	May 15
Crowberry	Empetrum nigrum	Le Buttereau Trail	May 17
Kidney–leaved Violet	Viola renifolia	Warren Lake Trail	May 19
Golden Saxifrage	Chrysosplenium americana	Warren Lake Trail	May 19
American Fly Honeysuckle	Lonicera canadensis	McIntosh Brook Trail	May 20
Bunchberry	Cornus canadensis	McIntosh Brook Trail	May 20
Selkirk's Violet	Viola selkirkii	McIntosh Brook Trail	May 20
Blue Violet	Viola septentrionalis	Lone Shieling Trail	May 20
Dog–Violet	Viola conspersa	Lone Shieling Trail	May 20
Yellow Violet	Viola eriocarpa	Lone Shieling Trail	May 20
Toothwort	Dentaria diphylla	Lone Shieling Trail	May 20
Common Winter Cress	Barbarea vulgaris	Lone Shieling Trail	May 20
Small White Violet	Viola pallens	Middle Head Trail	May 21
Goldthread	Coptis trifolia	Lone Shieling Trail	May 23
Red Elderberry	Sambucus pubens	Grande Anse	May 24
Red Baneberry	Actacaea rubra	Chéticamp	May 25

Blue Violet	Viola cucullata	Chéticamp	May 25
English Plantain	Plantago lanceolata	Chéticamp	May 25
Pin–Cherry	Prunus pensylvanica	Chéticamp	May 25
Shadbush	Amelanchier laevis	Chéticamp	May 25
Amelanchier	Amelanchier Bartramiana	Clyburn Valley Trail	May 25
Pussy–toes	Antennaria canadensis	Chéticamp	May 26
Sarsaparilla	Aralia nudicaulis	Chéticamp	May 26
Dewberry	Rubus pubescens	Chéticamp	May 26
Starflower	Trientalis borealis	Chéticamp	May 26
Wild Lily–of–the -Valley	Maianthemum canadense	Chéticamp	May 26
Skunk Current	Ribes glandulosum	Chéticamp	May 26
Sugar Maple	Acer saccharum	Chéticamp	May 26
Clintonia	Clintonia borealis	Chéticamp	May 26
Kidney–leaved Buttercup	Ranunculus abortivus var.	Chéticamp	May 26
Thyme–leaved Speedwell	Veronica serpyllifolia	Chéticamp	May 26
Mouse–eared Chickweed	Cerastium vulgatum	Chéticamp	May 26
Smooth Gooseberry	Ribes hirtellum	Presqu'île	May 27
Starry False Solomon's Seal	Smilacina stellata var.	Presqu'île	May 27
Purple Avens	Geum rivale	Le Buttereau Trail	May 27
Seashore–Plantain	Plantago juncoides	Le Buttereau Trail	May 27
Sea Milkwort	Glaux maritima	Le Buttereau Trail	May 27
Sheep sorrel	Rumex acetosella	Le Buttereau Trail	May 27
Shepherdia	Shepherdia canadensis	Le Buttereau Trail	May 27
Pale Laurel	Kalmia polifolia	Fishing Cove Lake Trail	May 29
Hare's Tale	Eriophorum spissum	Fishing Cove Lake Trail	May 29
Green–Twisted Stalk	Streptopus amplexifolius	Fishing Cove Lake Trail	May 29
Bog Rosemary	Andromeda glaucophylla	Fishing Cove Lake Trail	May 29
Rhodora	Rhododendron canadense	Fishing Cove Lake Trail	May 29
Bakeapple	Rubus chamaemorus	Fishing Cove Lake Trail	May 29
Bastard Toad–flax	Comandra richardsiana	Fishing Cove Lake Trail	May 29
Nodding Trillium	Trillium cernuum	La Prairie Trail	May 30
Blueberry	Vaccinium angustifolium	Chéticamp	May 30
White Ash	Fraxinus americana	La Prairie Trail	May 30
Bog Buckbean	Menyanthes trifoliata	French Mtn. Bog Trail	May 30
Red Oak	Quercus borealis	Chéticamp	May 30
Hawthorn	Crataegus sp.	Chéticamp	May 30
Cow parsnip	Heracleum lanatum	L'Acadien Trail	May 31
Miterwort	Mitella nuda	L'Acadien Trail	May 31
Tall Meadow Rue	Thalictrum polygamum	L'Acadien Trail	May 31
Yellow Avens	Geum aleppicum	L'Acadien Trail	May 31
Striped Maple	Acer pensylvanicum	L'Acadien Trail	May 31
Wild red currant	Ribes triste	L'Acadien Trail	May 31
Spurrey	Spergularia marina	North Bay Office	June 1

Silverweed	Potentilla anserina	Petit Étang Beach	June 1
Beach Pea	Lathyrus japonicus	Petit Étang Beach	June 1
Arenaria	Arenaria lateriflora	Petit Étang Beach	June 1
Tall Buttercup	Ranunculus acris	Chéticamp	June 1
Yarrow	Achillea lanulosa	Chéticamp	June 1
Rose Yarrow	A. millefolium f. rosea	Chéticamp	June 1
Three–toothed cinquefoil	Potentilla tridentata	Trous de Saumon Trail	June 2
Twinflower	Linnaea borealis	Trous de Saumon Trail	June 2
False Solomon's Seal	Smilacina racemosa	Trous de Saumon Trail	June 2
Wood Sorrel	Oxalis montana	Trous de Saumon Trail	June 2
Creeping Buttercup	Ranunculus repens	Trous de Saumon Trail	June 2
Mouse–ear Hawkweed	Hieracium	Trous de Saumon Trail	June 2
Herb–Robert	Geranium robertianum	Trous de Saumon Trail	June 2
Round–leaved Dogwood	Cornus rugosa	Trous de Saumon Trail	June 2
Red–osier	Cornus stolonifera	Trous de Saumon Trail	June 2
Blueberry	Vaccimium brittonii	Trous de Saumon Trail	June 2
Hawthorn	Crataegus densiflora	Trous de Saumon Trail	June 2
Red Clover	Trifolium pratense	Chéticamp	June 3
Labrador tea	Ledum groenlandicum	Skyline Trail	June 3
Common Speedwell	Veronica officinalis	Skyline Trail	June 3
Chokeberry	Aronia sp.	Skyline Trail	June 3
False Holly	Nemopanthus mucronata	Skyline Trail	June 3
Choke–cherry	Prunus virginiana	Le Buttereau Trail	June 6
Ox–eyed Daisy	Chrysanthemum leucanth.	Le Buttereau Trail	June 6
Water Cress	Nasturtium officinale	Benjie's Lake Trail	June 7
Yellow Pond Lily	Nuphar rubrodiscum	Chéticamp	June 7
Common Lady Slipper	Cypripedium acaule	Benjie's Lake Trail	June 7
Orange Hawkweed	Hieracium aurantiacum	Benjie's Lake Trail	June 7
Large Cranberry	Vaccinium macrocarpon	Benjie's Lake Trail	June 7
Pitcher plant	Sarracenia purpurea	Benjie's Lake Trail	June 10
3–leaf False Solomon's Seal	Smilacina trifolia	Benjie's Lake Trail	June 10
Lupine	Lupinus polyphyllus	North Mountain	June 10
Rough Cinquefoil	Potentilla norvegica	Grande Falaise	June 11
King devil	Hieracium pratense	Grande Falaise	June 11
Common Blue–eyed grass	Sisyrinchium montanum	Chéticamp	June 11
Caraway	Carum carvi	Chéticamp	June 11
Blue Flag	Iris versicolor	Chéticamp	June 11
Blue Iris	Iris hookeri	Le Buttereau Beach	June 11
Sea Lungwort	Mertensia maritima	Chéticamp	June 11
Cow Vetch	Vicia cracca	Chéticamp	June 11
Blueberry	Vaccinium myrtilloides	Benjie's Lake Trail	June 11
Curled Dock	Rumex crispus	Presqu'île	June 12
Mountain Maple	Acer spicatum	Corney Brook	June 12

144

Black Snakeroot	Sanicula marilandica	Corney Brook	June 12
Mountain Ash	Sorbus americana	Corney Brook	June 12
Marsh Bedstraw	Galium palustre	Corney Brook	June 12
Sweet Cicely	Osmorhiza Claytoni	Corney Brooik	June 12
Sweet Cicely	Osmorhiza chilensis	McIntosh Brook	June 12
Hooked Crowfoot	Ranunculus recurvatus	Corney Brook	June 12
Early Coralroot	Corallorhiza trifida	Corney Brook	June 12
Black Medic	Medicago lupulina	Chéticamp	June 15
Wild Raspberry	Rubus strigosus	Le Buttereau Trail	June 15
Heal All	Prunella vulgaris	Chéticamp	June 15
Broad leaved Twayblade	Listera convallarioides	McIntosh Brook	June 16
False Solomon's Seal	Smilacina racemosa	McIntosh Brook	June 16
Pink Pyrola	Pyrola asarifolia	McIntosh Brook	June 16
Wild Raisin	Viburnum cassinoides	French Mtn. Bog Trail	June 16
Arethusa	Arethusa bulbosa	French Mtn. Bog Trail	June 16
Sea Rocket	Cakile edentula	Presqu'île	June 16
Common Blackberry	Rubus allegheniensis	Chéticamp	June 16
Yellow Goatsbeard	Tragopogon pratensis	Chéticamp	June 16
Green Habenaria	Habenaria hyperborea	Chéticamp	June 20
White Baneberry	Actaea Pachypoda	McIntosh Brook	June 21
Canada Anemone	Anemone canadensis	La Prairie Trail	June 21
Small Sundrop	Oenothera perennis	La Prairie Trail	June 21
Hare Bell	Campanula rotundifolia	Headlands	June 23
Yellow Rattle	Rhinanthus crista–galli	Headlands	June 23
Forget–me–not	Myosotis laxa	Le Buttereau Trail	June 23
Grove Sandwort	Arenaria lateriflora	Headlands	June 23
Bedstraw	Galium tinctorium	Chéticamp	June 23
One–flowered Pyrola	Moneses uniflora	L'Acadien Trail	June 23
Dusty Miller	Artemisia stelleriana	Presqu'île	June 25
Large–leaved Avens	Geum macrophyllum	L'Acadien Trail	June 25
Pussy toes	Antenaria sp.	L'Acadien Trail	June 27
Bush Honeysuckle	Diervilla lonicera	L'Acadien Trail	June 28
Evening Primrose	Oenothera biennis	Chéticamp	June 29
Large Round–leaved Orchid	Habenaria obiculata	McIntosh Brook Trail	June 29
Spotted Coralroot	Corallorhiza maculata	McIntosh Brook Trail	June 29
Cow Wheat	Melampyrum lineare	Jack Pine Trail	June 30
Pearly Everlasting	Anaphalis margaritacea	Chéticamp	July 2
Willow Herb	Epilobium adenocaulon	Chéticamp	July 2
Muskflower	Mimulus moschatus	Chéticamp	July 2
Joe Pye–weed	Eupatorium maculatum	Chéticamp	July 2
Shrubby Cinquefoil	Potentilla fruticosa	Chéticamp	July 2
White Bog–orchid	Habenaria delatata	Chéticamp	July 2
Golden Heather	Hudsonia ericoides	Skyline Trail	July 2

Lambkill	Kalmia augustifolia	Skyline Trail	July 2
Musk Mallow	Malva moschata	Chéticamp	July 3
Spreading Dogbane	Apocynum androsaemifoli.	Chéticamp	July 3
Swamp Rose	Rosa nitida	Chéticamp	July 3
White Sweet Clover	Melilotus alba	Chéticamp	July 3
Black Knapweed	Centaurea nigra	Chéticamp	July 5
Bitter Dock	Rumex obtusifolius	Chéticamp	July 5
Partridge Berry	Mitchella repens	Chéticamp	July 5
Swamp Ragwort	Senecio robbinsii	Margaree	July 6
White–Fringed Orchid	Habenaria blephariglottis	French Mtn. Bog Trail	July 6
Ragwort	Senecio jacobaea	Chéticamp	July 7
Northern Willow Herb	Epilobium glandulosum	Chéticamp	July 7
Lion's Paw	Prenanthes trifoliolata	Chéticamp	July 7
Wild Basil	Satureja vulgaris	Chéticamp	July 7
Butter–and–Eggs	Linaria vulgaris	Roadsides	July 7
Dwarf Enchanter Nightshade	Circaea alpina	La Prairie Trail	July 7
Enchanter's Nightshade	Circaea quadrisulcata	La Prairie Trail	July 7
Meadowsweet	Spiraea latifolia	La Prairie Trail	July 7
Marsh Cinquefoil	Potentilla palustris	La Prairie Trail	July 7
Cat–tail	Typha angustiflia	La Prairie Trail	July 7
Canadian Burnet	Sanguisorba canadensis	La Prairie Trail	July 7
Fall Dandelion	Leontodon autumnalis	Robert Brook	July 7
Yellow Wood–sorrel	Oxalis stricta	Robert Brook	July 7
Daisy Fleabane	Erigeron annuus	Robert Brook	July 7
Swamp Thistle	Cirsium muticum	Robert Brook	July 7
Tansy	Tanacetum vulgare	Cabot Trail	July 7
Wild Thyme	Thymus serpyllum	Chéticamp	July 7
Wild Vetch	Vicia augustifolia	Corney Brook	July 8
Sneezeweed Yarrow	Achillea ptarmica	Corney Brook	July 8
Flat–topped Aster	Aster umbellatus	Chéticamp	July 9
Common St. John's Wort	Hypericum perforatum	Chéticamp	July 9
Fireweed	Epilobium augustifulium	Chéticamp	July 9
Small spearwort	Ranunculus reptans	Chéticamp	July 9
Swamp Candle	Lysimachia terrestris	Chéticamp	July 9
Blue–eyed Grass	Sisyrinchium augustifolia	Chéticamp	July 9
Wild Rose	Rosa virginiana	Chéticamp	July 9
Bugleweed	Lycopus uniflorus	Chéticamp	July 9
Rare Bur–reed	Sparganium minimum	Chéticamp	July 9
Pale St. John's Wort	Hypericum ellipticum	Chéticamp	July 9
Canada Hawkweed	Hieracium canadense	Chéticamp	July 9
New York Aster	Aster novi–belgii	Chéticamp	July 9
Canada Goldenrod	Solidago canadensis	Chéticamp	July 9
Staghorn Sumach	Rhus typhina	Chéticamp	July 9

Rough–fruited Cinquefoil	Potentilla recta	Chéticamp	July 11
Lesser stitchwort	Stellaria graminea	Chéticamp	July 11
Bog Aster	Aster nemoralis	Fishing Cove Lake Trail	July 11
Bog Goldenrod	Solidago uliginosa	French Mtn. Bog Trail	July 11
Rose Pogonia	Pogonia ophioglossoides	French Mtn. Bog Trail	July 11
Creeping buttercup	Ranunculus repens	McIntosh Brook	July 11
Tall White Lettuce	Prenanthus altissima	McIntosh Brook	July 11
Shinleaf	Pyrola elliptica	McIntosh Brook	July 11
Bladderwort	Utricularia cornuta	French Mtn. Bog Trail	July 11
One–sided Wintergreen	Pyrola secunda	McIntosh Brook	July 11
Common Mullein	Verbascum thapsus	MacKenzie Mountain	July 11
Silver-rod	Solidago bicolor	Chéticamp	July 11
Chéticamp Goldenrod	S. bicolor XS. canadensis	Chéticamp Bridge	July 11
Cranberry	Vaccinium macrocarpon	Bogs	July 11
Round–leaved Sundew	Drosera rotundifolia	Bogs	July 13
Common Eyebright	Euphrasia americana	Presqu'île	July 13
Wild Morning–glory	Convolvulus sepium	Presqu'île	July 13
Sow–thistle	Sonchus arvensis	Presqu'île	July 13
Indian Cucumber–root	Mediola virginiana	Grande Anse	July 14
Arnica	Arnica chionopappa	Grande Anse	July 14
Willowherb	Epilobium hornemanni	Grande Anse	July 14
Arnica	Arnica lonchophylla ssp. chionopappa	Grande Anse	July 14
Columbine	Aquilegia vulgaris	Dingwall	July 14
Canada Thistle	Circium arvense	Cabot Trail	July 15
Deptford Pink	Dianthus armeria	Cabot Trail	July 15
Cat's Ear	Hypochoeris radicata	Dingwall	July 15
Bird's–foot Trefoil	Lotus corniculatua	Chéticamp	July 16
Ragged–Fringed Orchid	Habenaria lacera	Chéticamp	July 16
Shepherd's Purse	Capsella bursa–pastoris	Chéticamp	July 16
Woodland Aster	Aster acuminatus	McIntosh Brook	July 16
Agrimony	Agrimonia gryposepala	Corney Brook	July 16
Chicory	Cichorium intybus	Corney Brook	July 16
Indian Pipe	Monotropa uniflora	Corney Brook	July 16
Fringed–Orchid	Habenaria fimbriate	Corney Brook	July 16
Calico Aster	Aster lateriflorus	Corney Brook	July 16
Pondweed	Potamogeton pectinatus	Dingwall	July 16
Black–eyed Susan	Rudbeckia serotina	Chéticamp	July 18
Bull Thistle	Cirsium vulgare	Chéticamp	July 18
Flat–Topped Aster	Aster umbellatus	La Prairie Trail	July 20
Panicled Aster	Aster simplex	La Prairie Trail	July 20
New England Aster	Aster novae–angliae	La Prairie Trail	July 20
New York Aster	Aster novi–belgii	La Prairie Trail	July 20

Joe Pye–weed	Eupatorium maculatum	La Prairie Trail	July 20
Small Purple–fringed Orchid	Habenaria psycodes	La Prairie Trail	July 20
Wild Mint	Mentha arvensis	La Prairie Trail	July 20
Scotch Lovage	Ligusticum scothicum	La Prairie Trail	July 20
Green Wood Orchis	Havenaria clavellata	French Lake	July 21
Nodding Ladies' Tresses	Spiranthes cernua	Bogs	July 23
Heart–leaved Aster	Aster cordifolius	Benjie's Lake Trail	July 23
Yellow–eyed Grass	Xyris montana	Boggy barrens	July 23
Nodding Ladies' Tresses	Spiranthes lacera	Boggy barrens	July 23
Virgin's Bower	Clematis virginiana	Chéticamp	July 25
Hemp Nettle	Galeopsis tetrahit	Chéticamp	July 27
Orach	Atriplex patula	Le Buttereau Trail	July 31
Sow–Thistle	Sonchus oleraceus	Le Buttereau Trail	July 31
Common Burdock	Aretium minus	Le Buttereau Trail	July 31
Lesser Daisy Fleabane	Erigeron strigosus	Le Buttereau Trail	July 31
Pipewort	Eriocaulon septangulare	Benjie's Lake Trail	Aug. 1
Water Lobelia	Lobelia dortmanna	Benjie's Lake Trail	Aug. 1
Fragrant White Water–Lily	Nymphaea odorata	Freshwater Lake	Aug. 2
Rough Stemmed Goldenrod	Solidago rugosa	Le Buttereau Trail	Aug. 5
Narrow–leaved Goldenrod	Solidago graminifolia	Le Buttereau Trail	Aug. 5
Rough Hawkweed	Hieracium scabrum	Le Buttereau Trail	Aug. 5
Pinweed	Lechea intermedia var.	Le Buttereau Trail	Aug. 8
Bittersweet	Solanum dulcamare		Aug. 11
Tearthumb	Polygonum sagittatum	Lac Trail	Aug. 16
Pale Touch–me–not	Impatiens pallida	Lac Trail	Aug. 16
St. John's Wort	Hypericum boreale	Lac Trail	Aug. 16
Tall Needle	Urtica procera	Lac Trail	Aug. 16
Seaside Goldenrod	Solidago sempervirens	Chéticamp	Aug. 16
Beechdrops	Epifagus virginiana	Chéticamp	Aug. 29
Zigzag Goldenrod	Solidago flexicaulis	Skyline Trail	Sep. 10

PLANT LIST

The following up-to-date list of all bryophytes and vascular plants is arranged in a botanical fashion because many of the plants have only Latin names. When there is a common name, both are listed.

Index to the plant list:

Trees: 150, 156, 157, 160, 161, 164
Shrubs: 150, 156 - 164, 166
Ferns: 149, 150, 153
Grasses: 151, 152
Flowers: 154 - 168
Mosses & Liverworts: 169 - 173
Lichens: 175 - 177
Sedges: 154

LATIN NAME	COMMON NAME	LATIN NAME	COMMON NAME
EQUISETUM		ISOETES	QUILLWORTS
arvense	Field horsetail	muricata	Quillwort
fluviatile	Water horsetail	macrospara	Quillwort
hyemale	Scouring rush	Tuckermani	Quillwort
variegatum			
scirpoides	Dwarf scouring rush	BOTRYCHIUM	GRAPE-FERN
sylvaticum	Wood horsetail	multifidum	Grape-fern
		dissectum	Grape-fern
LYCOPODIUM		Lunaria	Moonwort
Selago	Fir Club-moss	simplex	Grape-fern
lucidulum	Shining Club-moss	matricariaefolium	
inundatum	Bog Club-moss	lanceolatum	Grape-fern
annotinum	Bristly Club-moss	virginianum	Rattlesnake fern
clavatum	Club-Moss		
obscurum	Ground Pine	OSMUNDA	
sabinaefolium	Club-moss	regalis	Royal Fern
flabelliforme	Club-moss	Claytoniana	Interrupted Fern
tristachyum	Club-moss	cinnamomea	Cinnamon Fern
SELAGINELLA		SCHIZAEA	
Selaginoiges		pusilla	Curly Grass Fern

LATIN NAME	COMMON NAME	LATIN NAME	COMMON NAME
WOODSIA		ASPLENIUM	
alpina	Alpine Woodsia	viride	Green spleenwort
ilvensis	Rusty Woodsia	Trichomanes	Spleenwort
glabella	Smooth Woodsia		
		ADIANTUM	
CYSTOPTERIS	BLADDER FERNS	pedatum	Maidenhair fern
fragilis	Common Bladder fern		
bulbifera	Bulblet fern	PTERIDIUM	
		aquilinum	Bracken
PTERETIS			
pensylvanica	Ostrich fern	POLYPODIUM	
		virginianum	Rock polypody
ONOCLEA			
Sensibilis	Sensitive fern	TAXUS	
		canadensis	Yew
DRYOPTERIS			
Thelypteris	Marsh fern	ABIES	
noveboracensis	New York fern	balsamea	Balsam fir
disjuncta	Oak fern		
Phegopteris	Beech fern	TSUGA	
spinulosa	Wood fern	canadensis	Hemlock
intermedia	Wood fern		
cristata	Crested Wood fern	PICEA	SPRUCE
Filix-mas	Male fern	glauca	White spruce
marginalis	Marginal fern	rubens	Red spruce
fragrans	Fragrant fern	mariana	Black spruce
POLYSTICHUM		LARIX	LARCH
Lonchitis	Holly fern	laricina	Tamarack
Braunii	Holly fern		
acrostichoides	Christmas fern	PINUS	PINE
		Strobus	White pine
DENNSTAEDTIA		resinosa	Red pine
punctilobula	Hay-scented fern	Banksiana	Jack pine
ATHYRIUM		JUNIPERUS	
thelypterioides	Silvery spleenwort	communis	Common Juniper
Filix-femina	Lady fern	horizontalis	Creeping Juniper
		TYPHA	CAT-TAIL

LATIN NAME	COMMON NAME	LATIN NAME	COMMON NAME
latifolia	Broad-leaved	ZANNICHELLIA	
angustifolia	Narrow-leaved	palustris	Horned pondweed
SPARGANIUM	BUR-REED	NAJAS	
eurcarpum	Giant bur-reed	flexilis	Naiad
americanum	Bur-reed		
chlorocarpum	Bur-reed	TRIGLOCHIN	
angustifolium	Bur-reed	elata	Arrow-grass
multipedunculatum	Bur-reed	palustris	Marsh arrow-grass
minimum	Bur-reed		
hyperboreum	Bur-reed	SCHEUCHZERIA	
		palustris	Arrow-grass
ZOSTERA			
marina	Eel-grass	SAGITTARIA	ARROW-HEAD
		graminea	Arrow-head
POTAMOGETON	PONDWEED	latifolia	Arrow-head
filiformis	Pondweed	cureata	Arrow-head
pectiatus	Sago pond-weed		
Robbinsii	Pondweed	VALLISNERIA	
confervoides	Pondweed	americana	Tape-grass
zosteriformis	Pondweed		
pusillus	Pondweed	BROMUS	BROME GRASS
obtusifolius	Pondweed	ciliatus	Brome grass
Berchtoldi	Pondweed	mollis	Soft Chess
Spirillus	Pondweed		
epihydrus	Pondweed	SCHIZACHNE	
alpinus	Pondweed	purpurascens	False Melic
amplifolius	Pondweed		
gramineus	Pondweed	FESTUCA	
natans	Pondweed	rubra	Red Fescue
Oadesianus	Pondweed	prolifera	Fescue
praelongus	Pondweed	elatior	Meadow Fescue
Richardsonii	Pondweed		
perfoliatus	Pondweed	PUCCINELLIA	
filiformis		americana	Salt-marsh grass
obtusifolius		pumila	Salt-marsh grass
zosteriformis			
		GLYCERIA	MANNA-GRASS
RUPPIA		borealis	Northern
maritima	Ditch-grass	canadensis	Rattlesnake-grass

LATIN NAME	COMMON NAME	LATIN NAME	COMMON NAME
striata	Fowl Manna-grass	SPHENOPHOLIS	
grandis	Reed Manna-grass	intermedia	Slender wedge-grass
Fernaldii	Small Manna		
		TRISETUM	
POA	BLUEGRASS	spicatum	
annua	Annual bluegrass	melicoides	
compressa	Canada bluegrass	triflorum	
pratensis	Kentucky bluegrass		
trivialis	Rough-stalked	AVENA	
sauluensis		fatua	Wild oats
alsodes			
nemoralis	Wood bluegrass	DESCHAMPSIA	
palustris	Meadow-grass	flexuosa	Hair-grass
alpina		caespitosa	
glaucantha			
		DANTHONIA	
DACTYLIS		spicata	Wire-grass
glomerata	Orchard-grass		
		CALAMAGROSTIS	
CYNOSURUS		Pickeringii	
cristatus	Crester Dog's-tail	canadensis	Blue-joint grass
		inexpansa	
DISTICHLIS		neglecta	
Spicata	Seashore salt-grass		
		AMMOPHILA	
PHRAGMITES		breviligulata	Beach grass
communis	Common reed		
		AGROSTIS	Bentgrass
AGROPYRON		alba	Red-top
trachycaulum	Slender wheat-grass	palustris	Creeping bent-grass
pugens		tenuis	Brown top
repens	Couch-grass	scabra	Tickle-grass
		perennans	Perennial agrostis
HORDEUM		canina	Velvet bent-grass
jubatum	Fox-tail barley		
		CINNA	
ELYMUS		latifolia	Wood-reed
mollis	American dune-grass		
virginicus	Wild rye	PHLEUM	
		pratense	Timothy

LATIN NAME	COMMON NAME	LATIN NAME	COMMON NAME
alpinum	Mountain timothy	ECHINOCHLOA	
		crusgalli	Barnyard-grass
ALOPECURUS	Meadow fox-tail		
pratensis	Meadow fox-tail	DULICHIUM	
geniculatus	Water fox-tail	arundinaceum	
aequalis	Water fox-tail		
		ELEOCHARIS	SPIKE-RUSH
MUHLENBERGIA		parvula	
gomerata		pauciclora	
uniflora		obtusa	
		eryropoda	
BRACHYELYTRUM		elliptica	
erectum			
		SCIRPUS	BULLRUSH
ORYZOPSIS		cespitosus	
asperifolia	Rich-grass	hudsonianus	
		rufus	
MILIUM		subterminalis	
effisim		americanus	
		robustus	
SPARTIA		maritimus	
pectinata	Broad-leaf	rubrotinctus	
alterniflora	Cord-grass	cyperinus	
patens	Cord-grass	atrocinctus	
PHALARIS		ERIOPHORUM	COTTON-GRASS
arundinacea	Reed canary-grass	spissum	Hare's-tail
		tenellum	
ANTHOXANTHUM		angustifolium	
odoratum	Sweet vernal-grass	viridi-carinatum	
		gracile	
HIEROCHLOE		virginicum	
odorata	Sweet-grass		
		RHYNCHOSPORA	BEAK-RUSH
LEERSIA		alba	
oryzoides	Rice cut-grass	fusca	
		capillacea	
PANICUM	PANIC-GRASS		
boreale		CLADIUM	TWIG-RUSH
lanuginosum		mariscoides	

LATIN NAME	COMMON NAME	LATIN NAME	COMMON NAME
CAREX	SEDGES	limosa	
rosea		paupercula	
diandra		scabrata	
stipata		lasiocarpapa	
disperma		pallescens	
trisperma		gracillima	
Madkenziei		castanea	
canescena		arctata	
brunnescens		debilis	
Deweyana		capillaris	
exilis		conoidea	
interior		leptonervia	
Howei		flava	
atlantica		viridula	
muricata		pauciflora	
scoparia		Pseudo-cyperus	
projecta		lurida	
Crawfordii		Michauxiana	
silicea		folliculata	
hormathodes		intumescens	
adusta		retrosa	
aenea		rostrata	
leptalea		oligosperma	
scirpoidea		vesicaria	
pensylvanica		atratiformis	
communis		capillaris	
novae-angliae		miliaris	
deflexa		crinita	
tonsa		plantaginea	
pedunculata		scirpoidea	
aurea			
paleacea		ARISAEMA	
salina		Stewardsonii	Jack-in-the-pulpit
crinita			
aquatilis		CALLA	
nigra		palustris	Water arum
lenticularis			
stricta		ACORUS	
tortatratiformis		Calamus	Sweet flag
Buxbaumii			

LATIN NAME	*COMMON NAME*	*LATIN NAME*	*COMMON NAME*
SPIRODELA		ALLIUM	
polyrhiza		Schoenoprasum	Chives
LEMNA		LILIUM	
trisulca	Duckweed	canadense	Canada Lily
minor	Duckweed		
		CLINTONIA	
XYRIS		borealis	Bluebead
montana	Yellow-eyed-grass		
		SMILACINA	
ERIOCAULN		racemosa	False Solomons' seal
septangulare	Pipewort	stellata	Starry false Solomon's
		trifolis	Three-leaved
JUNCUS	RUSH		
bufonius	Toad-rush	MAIANTHEMUM	
trifidus		canadense	Wild lily of the valley
Gerardi			
tenuis		STREPTOPUS	
filiformis		amplexifolius	Green twisted stalk
effusus	Soft -rush	roseus	Rose twisted stalk
stygius			
nodosus		POLYGONATUM	
alpinus		pubescens	Solomon's seal
canadensis			
brevicaudatus		MEDEOLA	
militaris		virginiana	Indian Cucumber-root
articulatus			
pelocarpus		TRILLIUM	
		cernuum	Nodding Trillium
LUZULA	WOODRUSH		
spicata		SISYRINCHIUM	
acuminata		montanum	Blue-eyed Grass
parviflora			
multiflora	Common woodrush	IRIS	
		Hookeri	
TOFIELDIA		versicolor	Blue Flag
glutinosa	False asphodel	Pseudacorus	Yellow Iris
UVULARIA		CYPRIPEDIUM	
sessiliforia	Bellwort	Calceolus	Yellow Lady's Slipper

LATIN NAME	COMMON NAME	LATIN NAME	COMMON NAME
reginae	Showy Lady's Slipper	convallarioides	Twayblade
acaule	Lady's Slipper		
		CORALLORHIZA	
HABENARIA	FRINGED ORCHID	trifida	Early Coralroot
viridis		maculata	Spotted Coralroot
clavellata			
hyperborea	Green Habenaria	MALAXIS	
dilatata	White Bog-Orchid	unifolia	Adder's-mouth
Hookeri			
orbiculata		LIPARIS	
macrophylla		Loeselii	Twayblade
obtuata			
blephariglottis	White Fringed Orchid	SALIX	WILLOWS
lacera	Ragged Fringed Orchid	lucida	Shining Willow
psycodes	Purple Fringed Orchid	cordata	Heart-leaved Willow
fimbriata	Fringed Orchid	rigida	
		Bebbiana	Beaked Willow
POGONIA		discolor	Pussy-willow
ophioglossoides	Rose Pogonia	humilis	Small Pussy-willow
		POPULUS	
CALAPOGON		tremuloides	Trembling Aspen
puchellus	Calapogon	grandidentata	Large-toothed Poplar
		alba	White Poplar
ARETHUSA		nigra	Lombardy Poplar
bulbosa	Arethusa	balsamifera	Balsam Poplar
SPIRANTHES		MYRICA	
lacera	Ladies' tresses	Gale	Sweet Gale
cernua	Nodding Ladies tresses	pensylvanica	Bayberry
lucida	Shining Ladies tresses		
Romanzoffiana	Hooded Ladies tresses	CORYLUS	
		cornuta	Hazelnut
GOODYERA		OSTRYA	
tesselata		virginiana	Iron-wood
oglongifolia	Rattlesnake-Plantain		
repens		BETULA	
		alleghaniensis	Yellow Birch
LISTERA		papyrifera	Paper Birch
cordata	Twayblade		

LATIN NAME	*COMMON NAME*	*LATIN NAME*	*COMMON NAME*
cordifolia		OXYRIA	
borealis		digyna	Mountain-Sorrel
michauxii			
occidentalis		RUMEX	
pumila	Bog-Birch	alpinus	
glandulsa		orbiculatus	Water-Dock
		crispus	Curled Dock
ALNUS		obtusifolius	Blunt-Leaved Dock
crispa	Downy Alder	maritimus	
rugosa	Speckled Alder	Acetosella	Sheep-Sorrel
		Acetosa	Garden-Sorrel
FAGUS			
grandifolia	Beech	POLYGONUM	
		Raii	
QUERCUS		Fowleri	
borealis	Red Oak	aviculare	
robur	English Oak	arenastrum	
		natans	Water smartweed
ULMUS		lapathifolium	
americana	American Elm	scabrum	
		Hydropiper	Water pepper
HUMULUS		Persicaria	Lady's-thumb
Lupulus	Hops	sagittatum	Tear-thumb
		cilinode	
URTICA		Convolvulus	Wild buckwheat
gracilis	Nettle	cuspidatum	Japanesse Knotweed
procera	Tall Nettle		
dioica	Stinging Nettle	CHENOPODIUM	
		album	Lamb's Quarters
LAPORTEA			
canadensis	Wood-Nettle	ATRIPLEX	
		patula	Orach
COMANDRA			
Richardsiana	Bastard Toadflax	SALICORNIA	
		europaea	Glasswort
GEOCAULON	COMANDRA		
lividum	Northern Comandra	SUAEDA	
		maritima	Sea-Blite
ARCEUTHOBIUM		americana	
pusillum	Dwarf Mistletoe		

LATIN NAME	COMMON NAME	LATIN NAME	COMMON NAME
SALSOLA		variegatum	Cow-Lily
Kali	Common Saltwort		
		NYMPHAEA	
CLAYTONIA		odorata	Water-Lily
caroliniana	Spring-Beauty		
		BRASENIA	
SPERGULARIA		Schreberi	Water-shield
rubra	Sand-Spurrey		
marina		RANUNCULUS	BUTTERCUPS
canadensis	Seaside Sand-spurrey	trichophyllus	White Water Crowfoot
arvensis	Spurrey	Cymbalaria	Seashore-Buttercup
		Gmelini	Water-Crowfoot
SAGINA		reptans	Small Spearwort
procumbens	Pearlwort	abortivus	Wood Buttercup
		recurvatus	
ARENARIA		repens	Creeping Buttercup
lateriflora	Sandwort	acris	Tall Buttercup
peploides	Sandwort		
		THALICTRUM	
STELLARIA		polygamum	Meadow-rue
media	Common Chickweed		
graminea	Stitchwort	ANEMONE	
Alsine	Marsh-chickweed	riparia	
calycantha	Northern Starwort	canadensis	
		quinquefolia	Wood-Anemone
CERASTIUM			
vulgatum	Chickweed	CLEMATIS	
arvense	Field-chickweed	virginiana	Virgin's-Bower
SAPONARIA		CALTHA	
officinalis	Bouncing-Bet	palustris	Marsh-Marigold
SILENE	Moss-campion	COPTIS	
Acaulis		trifolia	Goldthread
DIANTHUS		ACTAEA	
Armeria	Deptford Pink	rubra	Red Baneberry
		pachypoda	White Baneberry
NUPHAR			
rubrodiscum	Yellow Pond-Lily		

LATIN NAME	*COMMON NAME*	*LATIN NAME*	*COMMON NAME*
SANGUINARIA		CARDAMINE	
canadensis	Bloodroot	pensylvanica	Bitter cress
		parviflora	
DICENTRA			
Cucullaria	Dutchman's Breeches	ARABIS	
		hirsuta	
CORYDALIS		Drummondi	
sempervirens	Pink cory-dalis		
		SARRACENIA	
DRABA		purpurea	Pitcher-plant
norvegica			
hirta		DROSERA	SUNDEWS
arabisans		intermedia	Narrow-leaved
		rotundifolia	Round-leaved
LEPIDIUM			
campestre	Field-peppergrass	TILLAEA	
virginicum	Peppergrass	aquatica	Pigmyweed
CAPSELLA		SEDUM	
Bursa-pastoris	Shepherd's purse	Telephium	Live-forever
		Rosea	Rose-root
CAKILE			
edentula	Sea-rocket	SAXIFRAGA	
		arizoides	Saxifrage
RAPHANUS		Aizoon	Saxifrage
raphanistrum	Wild radish		
		MITELLA	
SISYMBRIUM		nuda	Naked-Miterwort
officinale	Hedge-mustard		
		CHRYSOSPLENIUM	
ERYSIMUM		americanum	Golden saxifrage
cheiranthoides	Wormseed-mustard		
		PARNASSIA	
NASTURTIUM		parviflora	Grass-Of-Parnassus
officinale	Watercress		
		RIBES	
DENTARIA		hirtellum	Gooseberry
diphylla	Toothwort	lacustre	Bristly black currant
		glandulsum	Skunk-currant
		triste	Wild red currant

LATIN NAME	COMMON NAME	LATIN NAME	COMMON NAME
SPIRAEA		recta	
latifolia	Meadowsweet	norvegica	Rough cinquefoil
		anglica	
SORBARIA		Anserina	Silverweed
sorbifolia	False Spiraea		
		GEUM	AVENS
PYRUS		canadense	White Avens
Malus	Apple	laciniatum	
		aleppicum	
ARONIA		macrophyllum	
prunifolia	Choke-berry	rivale	Purple Avens
melanocarpa	Black Chokeberry		
		RUBUS	BRAMBLES
SORBUS		Chamaemorus	Bakeapple
americana	Mountain-Ash	pubescens	Dewberry
decora	Dogberry	strigosus	Wild raspberry
		hispidus	Trailing blackberry
AMELANCHIER		elegantulus	
Wiegandii	Shadbush	canadenis	
intermedia	Wild Pear	recurvicaulis	
laevis	Bilberry		
Bartramiana		AGRIMONIA	AGRIMONY
		gryposepala	
CRATAEGUS		striata	
Brunetiana	Hawthorn		
macrosperma	Hawthorn	SANGUISORBA	BURNET
densiflora	Hawthorn	canadensis	Canadian Burnet
succulenta	Hawthorn		
submollis		ROSA	ROSES
		nitda	Swamp-rose
FRAGARIA		virginiana	Common wild rose
virginiana	Strawberry		
vesca	Strawberry	PRUNUS	PLUMS & CHERRIES
		pensylvanica	Pin-cherry
POTENTILLA	CINQUEFOILS	virginiana	Choke-cherry
fruticosa	Shrubby cinquefoil	nigra	Canada Plum
tridentata	Three-toothed		
palustris	Marsh-cinquefoil	CYTISUS	
argentea	Silvery cinquefoil	scoparius	Scotch Broom
pensylvanica			

LATIN NAME	COMMON NAME	LATIN NAME	COMMON NAME
LUPINUS polyphyllus	Garden-Lupine	POLYGALA sanguinea	MILKWORT
TRIFOLIUM pratense repens agrarium procumbens	CLOVER Red clover Creeping white clover Hop-clover Low Hop-clover	EUPHORBIA Cyparissias polygonifolia	SPURGE Cypress spurge Seaside spurge
		CALLITRICHE verna anceps	WATER-STAR WORT
MELILOTUS alba	SWEET-CLOVER White sweet clover		
MEDICAGO sativa lupulina	MEDICK Alfalfa Black medick	EMPETRUM nigrum atropurpureum Eamesii	CROWBERRY Black crowberry Purple crowberry
OXYTROPIS johannensis		FLOERKEA proserpinacoide	FALSE MERMAID
VICIA angustifolia Cracca	VETCH Wild vetch Tufted vetch	RHUS typhina radicans	Staghorn sumach Poison Ivy
LATHYRUS japonicus palustris	PEA Beach Pea Wild pea	ILEX verticillata	HOLLY Winterberry
		NEMOPANTHUS mucronata	FALSE HOLLY False Holly
LINUM catharticum	FLAX Fairy-flax	ACER spicatum pensylvanicum saccharum rubrum	MAPLE Mountain Maple Striped Maple Sugar Maple Red Maple
MILLEGRANA Radiola	Tiny all-seed		
OXALIS montana stricta	WOOD-SORREL Wood-sorrel Yellow wood-sorrel	IMPATIENS capensis	TOUCH-ME-NOT Spotted touch-me-not
GERANIUM Robertianum	Herb-Robert	RHAMNUS alnifolia	BUCKTHORN Alder-leaved

LATIN NAME	COMMON NAME	LATIN NAME	COMMON NAME
PARTHENOCISSUS		EPILOBIUM	WILLOW-HERB
quinquefolia	Virginia creeper	angustifolium	Fireweed
		strictum	
MALVA	MALLOW	leptophyllum	Bog willow-herb
rotundifolia	Round-leaved mallow	nesophilum	
moschata	Musk-mallow	palustre	
		glanulosum	
HYPERICUM	ST. JOHN'S WORT	adenocaulon	Willow-herb
boreale		Hornemanni	
majus			
canadense		OENOTHERA	EVENING-PRIMROSE
virginicum		biennis	Evening-Primrose
		parviflora	Small-flowered
HUDSONIA		perennis	Sundrops
ericoiides	Hudsonia		
		CIRCAEA	
LECHEA	PINWEED	quadrisulcata	Enchanters-nightshade
intermedia	Pinweed	canadenses	
		alpina	
VIOLA	VIOLET		
cucullata	Blue violet	MYRIOPHYLLUM	WATER-MILFOIL
nephrophylla		alterniflorum	
septentrionalis		exalbescens	
Selkirkii		verticillatum	
pallens	Small white violet	tenellum	
incognita	White violet		
eriocarpa	Yellow violet	PROSERPINACA	MERMAID-WEED
consperas	Dog-violet	palustris	
labradorica			
tricolor	Johnny-jump-up	HIPPURIS	MARE'S-TAIL
		vulgaris	
SHEPHERDIA			
canadensis	Shepherdia	ARALIA	SARSAPARILLA
		racemosa	American Spikenard
LYTHRUM		hispida	Bristly Aralia
Salicaria	Purple Loosestrife	nudicaulis	Wild Sarsaparilla
LUDWIGIA		HYDROCOTYLE	
palustris		americana	Water-pennywort

LATIN NAME	*COMMON NAME*	*LATIN NAME*	*COMMON NAME*
SANICULA		rugosa	Round-leaved
marilandica	Black Snakeroot	alternifolia	Alternate-leaved
gregaria	Sanicle		
		CHIMAPHILA	
OSMORHIZA	SWEET-CICELY	umbellata	Prince's pine
Claytoni	Hairy sweet-cicely		
obtusa		MONESES	
chilenses		uniflora	One-flowered shinleaf
CICUTA	WATER-HEMLOCK	PYROLA	WINTERGREEN
bulbifera	Bulbous water-hem.	secunda	One-sided
maculata	Water-hemlock	minor	Small wintergreen
		virens	Green-flowered
CARUM		elliptica	Shinleaf
Carvi	Caraway	asarifolia	
SIUM		MONOTROPA	
sauave	Water-parsnip	uniflora	Indian-pipe
		Hypopithys	Pine-sap
LIGUSTICUM			
scothicum	Scotch Lovage	LEDUM	
		groenlandicum	Labrador-tea
COELOPLEURUM			
lucidum		RHODODENDRON	
		canadense	Rhodora
CONIOSELINUM			
chinense	Hemlock-parsley	KALMIA	
		angustifolia	Lambkill
ANGELICA		polifolia	Pale Laurel
atropurpurea	Purple angelica		
		PHYLLODOCE	
HERACLEUM		caerulea	
lanatum	Cow-parsnip		
		ANDROMEDA	Bog Rosemary
DAUCUS		glaucophylla	
Carota	Wild carrot		
		CHAMAEDAPHNE	
CORNUS	DOG-WOOD	calyculata	Leather leaf
canadensis	Bunchberry		
stolonifera	Red Osier Dog-wood		

LATIN NAME	COMMON NAME	LATIN NAME	COMMON NAME
EPIGAEA		GLAUX	
repens	Mayflower	mariltima	Sea-Milkwort
GAULTHERIA		LIMONIUM	
procumbens	Teaberry	Nashii	Sea-Lavender
hipidula	Snowberry		
		FRAXINUS	ASH
ARCTOSTAPHYLOS		americana	White Ash
Uva-ursi	Bearberry	nigra	Black Ash
GAYLUSSACIA		SYRINGA	
dumosa	Bog huckleberry	vulgaris	Lilac
baccata	Huckleberry		
		HALENIA	
VACCINIUM	BLUEBERRIES	deflexa	Spurred Gentian
uliginosum	Alpine whortleberry		
cespitosum	Dwarf bilberry	BARTONIA	
ovalifolium		paniculata	Screw-Stem
myrtilloides	Canada blueberry		
angustifolium		MENYANTHES	
boreale		trifoliata	Buckbean
Vitis-Idaea	Foxberry		
Oxycoccos	Small cranberry	NYMPHOIDES	
macrocarpon	Large cranberry	cordata	Floating-heart
DIAPENSIA		APOCYNUM	
lapponica		androsaemifolium	Spreading dogbane
		cannabinum	Indian hemp
PRIMULA			
laurentiana		CONVOLVULUS	
mistassinica	Primrose	sepium	Wild morning-glory
LYSIMACHIA		MYOSOTIS	
terrestris	Loosestrife	scorpioides	Forget-me-not
thrysiflora	Water loosestrife	laxa	Small forget-me-not
TRIENTALIS		MERTENSIA	
borealis	Star-flower	maritima	Sea-lungwort
		SCUTELLARIA	Skullcap

LATIN NAME	COMMON NAME	LATIN NAME	COMMON NAME
lateriflora		MIMULUS	
galericulata		ringens	Monkey-flower
		moschatus	Muskflower
NEPETA			
cataria	Catnip	VERONICA	SPEEDWELL
		serpyllifolia	Thyme-leaved
GLECHOMA		tenella	
hederacea	Ground-ivy	officinalis	Common Speedwell
		scutellata	Marsh-Speedwell
PRUNELLA		americana	American Brookline
vulgaris	Heal-all	arvensis	Field-Speedwell
GALEOPSIS		MELAMPYRUM	
Tetrahit	Hemp-nettle	lineare	Cow-wheat
SATUREJA		EUPHRASIA	
vulgaris	Basil	Randii	Small Eyebright
		canadensis	Eyebright
LYCOPUS		americana	Eyebright
uniflorus	Bugleweed		
americanus	Water-horehound	RHINANTHUS	
		Crista-galli	Yellow-rattle
MENTHA			
arvensis	Field-mint	PEDICULARIS	
		palustris	Swamp-Lousewort
SOLANUM			
Dulcamara	Bittersweet	EPIFAGUS	
nigrum	Black nightshade	virginiana	Beech-drops
VERBASCUM		OROBANCHE	
Thapsus	Common Mullein	uniflora	Broom-rape
LINARIA		UTRICULARIA	BLADDERWORT
vulgaris	Butter-and-Eggs	purpurea	
dalmaticla		geminiscapa	
		vulgais	
CHELONE		minor	
glabra	Turtlehead	intermedia	
		cornuta	

LATIN NAME	COMMON NAME	LATIN NAME	COMMON NAME
PINGUICULA		trilobum	Highbush-cranberry
vulgaris	Butterwort		
		SAMBUCUS	
PLANTAGO	PLANTAIN	canadensis	Common Elder
major	Broad-leaved	pubens	Red-berried Elder
juncoides	Seashore-plantain		
oliganthos	Seashore-plantain	ECHINOCYSTIS	
lanceolata	English plantain	lobata	Wild cucumber
LITTORELLA		CAMPANULA	
americana		rotundifolia	Harebell
GALIUM	BEDSTRAW	LOBELIA	
triflorum	Sweet-scented	inflata	Indian-tobacco
kamtschaticum	Northern bedstraw	Dortmanna	Water Lobelia
palustre	Common bedstraw		
tinctorium	Small bedstraw	EUPATORIUM	
labradoricum		macullatum	Joe-Pye-weed
asprellum	Rough bedstraw	perfoliatum	Boneset
MITCHELLA		SOLIDAGO	GOLDENROD
repens	Partridge-berry	flexicaulis	Wood-goldenrod
		macropylla	Large- leaved
HOUSTONIA		bicolor	Silverrod
caerulea	Bluets	puberula	Rough goldenrod
		multiradiata	
DIERVILLA		sempervirens	Seaside goldenrod
Lonicera	Bush honeysuckle	juncea	Early goldenrod
		uliginosa	Bog-goldenrod
LONICERA		rugosa	Rough goldenrod
villosa	Mtn. fly-honeysuckle	canadensis	Canada goldenrod
canadensis	Amer. fly-honeysuckle	gigantea	
LINNAEA		ASTER	
borealis	Twin-flower	cordifolius	Heart-leaved aster
		novae-angliae	New England aster
VIBURNUM		puriceus	Rough aster
alnifolium	Hobblebush	radula	Rough-leaved aster
cassinoides	Witherod	lateriflorus	
edule	Cranberrybush	simplex	

LATIN NAME	COMMON NAME	LATIN NAME	COMMON NAME
borealis		ACHILLEA	
novi-belgii		Ptarmica	Sneezeweed
nemoralis	Bog aster	borealis	
Blakei		lanulosa	Yarrow
acuminatus	Wood aster		
		ANTHEMIS	
ERIGERON	FLEABANE	Cotula	Chamomile
hyssopifolius			
annuus	Daisy-fleabane	MATRICARIA	
		maritima	Mayweed
ANTENNARIA	EVERLASTING	matricarioides	Pineapple-weed
canadensis	Pussy's toes		
neodioica	Everlasting	CHRYSANTHEMUM	
petaloidea		Leucanthemum	Ox-eye-daisy
ANAPHALIS		TANACETUM	
margaritacea	Pearly Everlasting	vulgare	Tansy
GNAPHALIUM		ARTEMISIA	WORMWOOD
uliginosum	Low Cudweed	canadensis	
sylvaticum		Stelleriana	Beach-wormwood
INULA		TUSSILAGO	
Helenium	Elecampane	Farfara	Coltsfoot
XANTHIUN		ARNICA	
echinatum	Cocklebur	angustifolia	
		chionopappa	
RUDBECKIA			
serotina	Black-eyed-Susan	ERECHTITES	
		hieracifolia	Fireweed
BIDENS			
cernua	Nodding bur-marigold	SENECIO	
tripartita	Swamp-beggar-ticks	vulgaris	Common groundsel
frondosa	Common beggar-ticks	sylvaticus	
hyperborea		Jacobaea	Stinking-willie
		pauperculus	
MEGALODONTA		Robbinsii	Swamp-ragwort
Beckii	Water-marigold	aureus	Golden ragwort

LATIN NAME	COMMON NAME	LATIN NAME	COMMON NAME
ARCTIUM		SONCHUS	
minus	Common burdock	arvensis	Perennial sow-thistle
		asper	Spiny sow-thistle
CIRSIUM	THISTLE		
vulgare	Bull thistle	LACTUCA	
muticum	Swamp-thistle	canadensis	Wild Lettuce
arvense	Canada thistle	biennis	Blue wild lettuce
CENTAUREA		PRENANTHES	
nigra	Black Knapweed	trifoliolata	Lion's paw
		altissima	
CICHORIUM			
Intybus	Common chicory	HIERACIUM	HAWKWEED
		Pilosella	Mouse-ear hawkweed
LEONTODON		aurantiacum	Devil's paint-brush
autumnalis	Fall-dandelion	caespitosum	Hawkweed
		floribundum	King-devil
TRAGOPOGON	Goat's Beard	piloselloides	
pratensis		murorum	Golden lungwort
		Lachenalii	
TARAXACUM		Robinsonii	
erythrospermum	Red-seeded dandelion	canadense	Canada hawkweed
officinale	Dandelion	scabrum	Rough hawkweed

MOSSES AND LIVERWORTS

Most of us don't think about mosses much. Instead we trample them inadvertently at almost every opportunity. Some campers even sleep on top of them. But mosses get revenge by being slippery while lying in wait under the water on the only rocks to walk across the brook on. Liverworts, on the other hand, are almost invisible to most people. But if you open your eyes wide when you're at the edge of a shaded wooded stream, you should see them. Look for small greenish plant-like leaves stuck to rocks or tree trunks. They slow rainwater runoff and help conserve topsoil.

To date, 292 mosses and liverworts have been identified here and their Latin and common names are summarized in the following list.

LATIN NAME	COMMON NAME	LATIN NAME	COMMON NAME
Abietinella abietina		Blindia acuta	
Amblystegium		Brachythecium	
serpens		acuminatum	Cedar Moss
Amphidium lapponicum		Brachythecium	
Amphidium mougeotii		albicans	Cedar Moss
Anacamptodon		Brachythecium	
splachnoides	Knothole Moss	campestre	Cedar Moss
Andreaea rupestris	Rock Moss	Brachythecium	
Anomodon attenuatus	Tree apron Moss	curtum	Cedar Moss
Anomodon rostratus	Tree apron Moss	Brachythecium	
Amomodon viticulosis	Tree apron Moss	digastrum	Cedar Moss
Atrichum altecristatum	Catherinea Moss	Brachythecium	
Atrichum crispum	Catherinea Moss	oxycladon	Cedar Moss
Atrichum oerstedianum	Catherinea Moss	Brachythecium	
Aulacomnium		plumosum	Cedar Moss
androgynum		Brachythecium	
Aulacomnium palustre		populeum	Cedar Moss
		Brachythecium	
Barbula convoluta	Little beard Moss	reflexum	Cedar Moss
Barbula fallax	Little beard Moss	Brachythecium	
Barbula unguicilata	Little beard Moss	rivulare	Cedar Moss
Bartramia ithyphylla	Apple Moss	Brachythecium	
Bartramia pomiformis	Apple Moss	rutabulum	Cedar Moss

LATIN NAME	COMMON NAME	LATIN NAME	COMMON NAME
Brachythecium		Cynodontium strumiferm	
salebrosum	Cedar Moss	Cyrtomnium hymenophylloides	
Brachythecium			
velutinym	Cedar Moss	Dichelyma capillaceum	Water Moss
Brotherella recurvans		Dichodontium	
Bryhnia graminicolor		pellucidum	
Bryhnis novoe-angliae		Dicranella cerviculata	Little Fork Moss
Bryoerythrophrophyllum		Dicranella grevilleans	Little Fork Moss
recurvirostrum		Dicranella heteromalla	Green Hair Moss
Bryum algovicum	Bryum Moss	Dicranella palustris	Little Fork Moss
Bryum caespiticium	Matted Bryum Moss	Dicranella subulata	Little Fork Moss
Bryum capillar	Bryum Moss	Dicranella varia	Little Fork Moss
Bryum lisae		Dicranoweisia crispula	
var. cuspisatum	Bryum Moss	Dicranum	
Bryum muehlenbeckii	Bryum Moss	condensatum	Fork Moss
Bryum pallescens	Bryum Moss	Dicranum flagellare	Whip Fork Moss
Bryum		Dicranum fulvum	Fork Moss
pseudotriquetrum	Bryum Moss	Dicranum fuscescens	Fork Moss
Bryum radiculosum	Bryum Moss	Dicranumn leioneuron	Fork Moss
Bryum stenotrichum	Bryum Moss	Dicranum majus	Fork Moss
Bryum weigelii	Bryum Moss	Dicranum montanum	Fork Moss
Buxbaumia aphylla	Hump-backed Elves	Dicranum ontariense	Fork Moss
Buxbaumia minakatae	Hump-backed Elves	Dicranum polysetum	Fork Moss
		Dicranum scoparium	Broom Moss
Callicladium haldanianum		Dicranum spurium	Fork Moss
Calliergon cordifoium	Schreiber's Moss	Dicranum undulatum	Wavy Broom Moss
Calliergon giganteum		Dicranum viride	Powder Gun Moss
Calliergon stramineum		Diphyscium foliosum	
Calliergonella cuspidata		Distichium capillaceum	
Campylium chrysophyllum		Ditrichum flexicaule	
Campylium hispidulum		Ditrichum lineare	
Campylium polygamum		Ditrichum pusillum	
Campylium radicale		Drepanocladus aduncus	
Campylium stellatum		Drepanocladus exannulatus	
Ceratodon purpureus	Horn-toothed Moss	Drepanocladus fluitans	
Climacium dendroides	Tree Moss	Drepanocladus revolvens	
Cratoneuron falcatum		Drepanocladus uncinatus	
Cratoneuron filicinum		Drepanocladus vernicosus	
Ctenidium malacodes		Drummondia prorepens	
Cynodontium alpestre			

LATIN NAME	COMMON NAME	LATIN NAME	COMMON NAME
Encalypta ciliata	Extinguisher Moss	Hygrohypnum ochraceum	
Encalypta procera	Extinguisher Moss	Hylocomium brevirostre	
Entodon concinnus	Glossy Entodon	Hylocomium	
Eurynchium pulchellum		splendens	Stair-step Moss
Eurynchium riparioides		Hylocmium umbratum	
		Hypnum cupressiforme	Feather Moss
Fissidens adianthoides	Maiden Hair Moss	Hypnum curvifolium	Feather Moss
Fissidens bryoides	Plume Moss	Hypnum fertile	Feather Moss
Fissidens cristatus	Plume Moss	Hypnum imponens	Feather Moss
Fissidens osmundoides	Plume Moss	Hypnum lindbergii	Feather Moss
Fontinalis antipyretica	Giant Fountain Moss	Hypnum pallescins	Feather Moss
Fontinalis dalecarlica	Brook Moss		
Fontinalis gigantea	Brook Moss	Isopterygiopsis mulleriana	
Fontinalis hypnoides	Brook Moss	Isopterygium elegans	
Fontinalis		Isopterygium pulchellum	
novae-angliae	Brook Moss	Isothecium stoloniferum	
Funaria hygrometrica	Cord Moss		
		Kiaeria blyttii	
Grimmia affinis	Beard Moss	Kiaeria starkei	
Gymnostomum			
aeruginosum	Twisted Moss	Leptobryum pyriforme	Thread Moss
Gymnostomim		Leptodictyum riparium	
recurvirostrum	Twisted Moss	Leskeella nervosa	
		Leucobrym glaucum	Pincushion Moss
Haplohymenium triste		Leucodon brachypus	Leucodon Moss
Hedwigia ciliata	Hedwig's Moss		
Helodium blandowii		Mnium ambiguum	
Herzogiella striatella		Mnium hornum	
Herzogiella turfacea		Mnium marginatum	
Heterocladium dimorphum		Mnium spinulosum	Flapper Moss
Homalia		Myurella julacea	
trichomanoides	Homalia Moss	Myurella sibirica	
Hygroamblystegium			
fluviatile		Neckera complanata	Feather Moss
Hygroamblystegium tenax		Neckera pennata	Feathered Neckera
Hygrohypnum bestii			
Hygrohypnum duriusculum		Oligotrichum hercynicum	
Hygrohypnum eugyrium		Oncophorus wahlenbergii	
Hygrohypnum luridum		Orthotrichum	
Hygrohypnum montanum		anomalum	Hair Tree Moss

171

LATIN NAME	COMMON NAME	LATIN NAME	COMMON NAME
Orthotrichum		Polytrichastrum ohioense	
obtusifolium	Hair Tree Moss	Polytrichum	
Orthotrichum		commune	Bird Wheat
sordidum	Hair Tree Moss	Polytrichum	
Orthotrichum		juniperinum	Juniper Moss
speciosum	Hair Tree Moss	Polytrichum piliferum	
Orthotrichum stellatum	Hair Tree Moss	Polytrichum strictum	
Oxystegus tenuirostre		Pseudobryum cinclidioides	
		Pseudoleskea patens	
Paludella squarrosa		Pseudoleskea stenophylla	
Paraleucobryum		Pterigyandrum filiforme	
longifolium		Ptilium	
Philonotis fontana	Aquatic Apple Moss	crista-castrensis	Knights Plume
Philonotis marchica	Aquatic Apple Moss	Pylaisiella intricata	
Plagiobryum zierii		Pylaisiella polyantha	
Plagiomnium ciliare		Pylaisiella selwynii	
Plagiomnium cuspidatum			
Planiomnium medium		Racomitrium aciculare	
Plagiopus oederiana		Racomitrium canescens	
Plagiothecium cavifolium		Racomitrium fasciculare	
Plagiothecium		Racomitrium heterostichum	
denticulatum	Cedar Moss	Racomitrium lanuginosum	
Plagiothecium laetum		Racomitrium microcarpon	
Platydictya confervoides		Racomitrium sudeticum	
Platydictya jungernannioides		Rhabdoweisia crispata	
Platydictya sublile		Rhizomnium appalachianum	
Platylomella lescurii		Rhizomnium magnifolium	
Pleurozium schreberi		Rhizomnium punctatum	
Pogonatum dentatum		Rhodobryum ontariense	
Pogonatum pensilvanicum		Rhytidiadelphus loreus	
Pogonatum urnigerum		Rhytidiadelphus subpinnatus	
Pohlia annotina	Nodding Moss	Rhytidiadelphus triquetrus	
Pohlia cruda	Nodding Moss	Rhytidium rugosum	
Pohlia filiformis	Nodding Moss		
Pohlia nutans	Nodding Moss	Saelania glaucescens	
Pohlia proligera	Nodding Moss	Schistidium apocarpum	
Pohlia wahlenbergii	Nodding Moss	Schistidium gracile	
Polytrichastrum		Schistidium maritimum	
alpinum		Schistidium rivulare	
Polytrichastrum formosum		Schistidium trichodon	

LATIN NAME	*COMMON NAME*	*LATIN NAME*	*COMMON NAME*
Schistostega pennata	Goblin Cave Moss	Sphagnum warnstorfii	Peat Moss
Scorpidium scorpioides		Sphagnum	
Seligeria diversifolia		ampullaceum	Peat Moss
Seligeria donniana			
Seligeria tristichoides		Tayloria serrata	
Sematophyllum		Tetraphis geniculata	
marylandicum		Tetraphis pellucida	
Sphagnum		Terraplodon angustatus	
angermanicum	Peat Moss	Tetraplodon mnioides	
Sphagnum		Tetrodontium brownianum	
capillifolium	Peat Moss	Thamnobryum	
Sphagnum centrale	Peat	alleghanisense	
Sphagnum compactum	Peat Moss	Thuidium delicatulum	Common Fern Moss
Sphagnum cuspidatum	Peat Moss	Thuidium recognitum	Fern Moss
Sphagnum fimbfriatum	Peat Moss	Timmia norvegica	
Sphagnum flavicomans	Peat Moss	Tomenthypnum nitens	
Sphagnum fuscum	Peat Moss	Tortella fragilis	
Sphagnum		Tortella humilis	
girgensohnii	Peat Moss	Tortella tortuosa	
Sphagnum imbricatum	Peat Moss	Tortula ruralis	Twisted Moss
Sphagnum lindbergii	Peat Moss	Trematodon ambiguus	
Sphagnum		Trichostomum crispulum	
magellanicum	Peat Moss		
Sphagnum majus	Peat Moss	Ulota coarctrata	Curled Leaf Moss
Sphagnum palustre	Reddish Peat Moss	Ulota crispa	Curled Leaf Moss
Sphagnum papillosum	Peat Moss	Ulota curvifolia	Curled Leaf Moss
Sphagnum pulchrum	Peat Moss	Ulota drummondii	Curled Leaf Moss
Sphagnum pylaesii	Peat Moss	Ulota hutchinsiae	Curled Leaf Moss
Sphagnum		Ulota phyllantha	Curled Leaf Moss
quinquefarium	Peat Moss		
Sphagnum recurvum	Peat Moss	Weissia controversa	
Sphagnum russowii	Peat Moss		
Sphagnum		Zygodon viridissimus	
squarrosum	Spread-leaved Peat		
Sphagnum			
subsecundum	Peat Moss		
Sphagnum tenillum	Peat Moss		
Sphagnum tenerum	Peat Moss		
Sphagnum teres	Peat Moss		
Sphagnum torreyanum	Peat Moss		

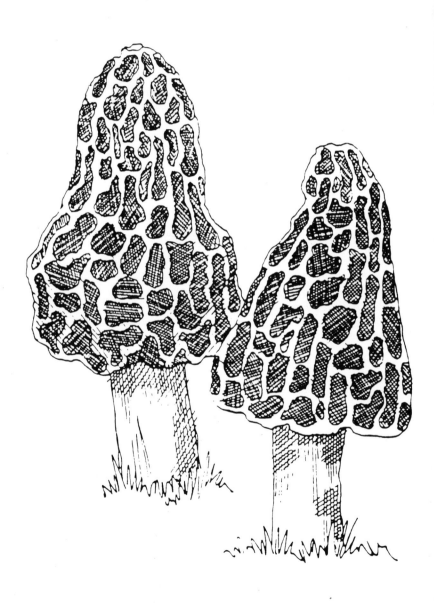

LICHENS

Lichens are very different from other plants. They are really two very different types of plants put together; fungi and algae blended only by nature's hand. Scientists have been able to take the two apart, but have never been able to put them back together again. They have been used by people for thousands of years as food, dyes and fire starters, to mention only a few. Today we use them to monitor air pollution, as they are very sensitive to man-made disturbances in our air. Lichens live for very long times; some colonies are estimated to be over 2,000 years old. You can take a walk on a rocky beach and tell by looking at the lichens when the last violent storm disturbed them. The following is a list of Latin and common names of the lichens found in northern Cape Breton.

LATIN NAME	COMMON NAME	LATIN NAME	COMMON NAME
Alectoria americans		Cladonia cornuta	
Alectoria implexa		Cladonia crispata	
Alectoria nigricans		Cladonia crispata	
Alectoria sarmentosa		var. virgata	
		Cladonia crispata	
Bacidia chlorantha		var. dilacerata	
Baeomyces roseus	Rosy Crust Lichen	Cladonia cristatella	British Soldier
Buellia punctata		Cladonia ecmocyna	
		Cladonia fimbriata	
Caloplaca flavovirescens		Cladonia furcata var.	
Caloplaca scopularis		racemosa	
Cetraria ciliaris		Cladonia gonache	
Cetraria ericetorum		Cladonia gracilis	
Cetraria glauca		var. gracilis	Spoon Lichen
Cetraira hepatizon		Cladonia gracilis	
Cetraria islandica	Iceland Moss Lichen	var. elongata	Spoon Lichen
Cetraria nivalis	Spanish Shield Lichen	Cladonia grayi	
Cetraria pinastri	Spanish Shield Lichen	Cladonia impexa ssp.	
Cladonia alpestris		laxiuscula	
Cladonia arbuscula		Cladonia mitis	
Cladonia boryi		Cladonia ochrochlora	
Cladonia cenotea		Cladonia papillaria	
Cladonia chlorophaea		Cladonia pleurota	

LATIN NAME	COMMON NAME	LATIN NAME	COMMON NAME
Cladonia pseudorangiformis		Melanaria macounii	
		Mycoblastus melinus	
Cladonia rangiferina	Reindeer Moss	Mycoblastus sanguinarius	
Cladonia scabriuscula			
Cladonia turgida		Nephroma arctricum	
Cladonia uncialis		Nephroma bellum	
Cladonia verticillata	Ladder Lichen	Nephroma lusitanicum	
Collelma subfurvum			
Cornicularia aculeata		Ochrolechia androgyna	
Cryocynia membrancea		Ochrolechia frigida	
		Ochrolechia tartarea	
Dermatocarpon miniatum			
		Pannaria pezizoides	
Lecanora cinerea	Manna Lichen	Parmelia centrifuga	Boulder Lichen
Lecanora glabrata	Manna Lichen	Parmelia conspersa	Boulder Lichen
Lecanora hypoptoides	Manna Lichen	Parmelia disjuncta	Boulder Lichen
Lecanora insignis	Manna Lichen	Parmelia glabratula	Boulder Lichen
Lecanora intricata	Manna Lichen	Parmelia incurva	Boulder Lichen
Lecanora laevata	Manna Lichen	Parmelia omphalodes	Boulder Lichen
Lecanora pallida	Manna Lichen	Parmelia omphalodes	
Lecanora symmicta	Manna Lichen	f. cinereoalbida	
Lecidea alborufescens		Parmelia panniformis	Boulder Lichen
Lecidea cinnaabarina		Parmelia physodes	Puffed Shield Lichen
Lecidea confluens		Parmelia physodes	
Lecidea crustulata		var. labrosa	
Lecidea cyanea		Parmelia saxatilis	Boulder Lichen
Lecidea granlosa		Parmelia sorediata	Boulder Lichen
Lecidea helvola		Parmelia stygia	Boulder Lichen
Lecidea lapicida		Parmelia subaurifera	Boulder Lichen
Lecidea plana		Parmelia tubulosa	Boulder Lichen
Lecidea recensa		Parmelia plumbea	Boulder Lichen
Lecidea tenebrosa		Parmelia hyperopta	Boulder Lichen
Lecidea vernalis		Peltigera canina	Dog-toothed Lichen
Lepraria incana		Peltigera leucophlebia	Toothed Lichen
Leptogium cyanescens		Peltigera membfranacea	Toothed Lichen
Leptogium cynaescens		Peltigera polydaactyla	Toothed Lichen
Leptogium saturninum		Peltigera scabrosa	Toothed Lichen
Lobaria pulmonaria	Lung Lichen	Pertusaria amara	
Lobaria quercizans	Speckled Lichen	Pertusaria laevigata	
Lobaria scrobiculata	Speckled Lichen		

LATIN NAME	COMMON NAME	LATIN NAME	COMMON NAME
Pertusaria nultipuncta		Stereocaulon	
Pertusaria veluta		tomentosum	Easter Lichen
Ramalina farinacea	Twig Lichen	Thelotream lepadinum	
Ramalina minuscula	Twig Lichen		
Ramalina pollinaria	Twig Lichen	Umbilicaria deusta	Rock Tripe
Rhizocarpon distinctum		Umbilicaria	
Rhizocarpon eupatraeum		hyperborea	Rock Tripe
Rhizocarpon geographicum		Umbilicaria	
		mammulata	Smooth Rock Tripe
Sarcogyne privigna		Umbilicaria	
Scrocogyne simplex		muehlenbergii	Rock Tripe
Sphaeorphorus fragilis		Umbilicaria papulosa	Blistered Rock Tripe
Sphaerophorus globosus		Umbilicaria polyphylla	Rock Tripe
Stereocaulon		Umbilicaria vellea	Fleecy Rock Tripe
cf. grande	Easter Lichen	Usnea dasypoga	Old Man's Beard
Stereocaulon coralloides		Usnea longissima	
var. spissum		var. laetevirens	
Stereocaulon			
dactylophyllum	Easter Lichen	Verrucaria acrotella	
Stereocaulon		Verrucaria erichsenii	
evolutoides	Easter Lichen	Verrucaria umbrinula	
Stereocaulon paschale			
f. colligatum		Xanthoria polycarpa	Yellow Wall Lichen

FUNGI: MUSHROOMS

Fungi play a major role in the renewal of the forest by decomposing organic matter, like leaves and logs. Some decompose dead animals, while others invade and sometimes kill living plants and animals. Experts in the field think that there may be as many different species of fungi in Nova Scotia as there are of all the other plants put together. However, the research is not clear yet as to which fungi might live around the Cabot Trail. The following list includes just a few of the bigger fungi, commonly called mushrooms.

Ivo Polach prepared the following list of 113 common mushrooms for Cape Breton Highlands National Park. Most mushrooms do not have common names, therefore, the list includes Latin names only. The letters after the names refer to the following information:

?	not known	x	not edible
e	edible	XX	deadly poison
ex	edible, excellent	EN	edible, not recommended

NON-GILLED MUSHROOMS

Albatrellus ovinus	e	Hericium coralloises	ex
Aleuria aurantia	e	Hydnellum scrobiculatum	EN
Boletus affinis	e	Hydnum repandum	ex
Boletus edulis	ex	Hydnum umbillicatum	e
Boletus huronensis	e	Hypomyces lactifluorum	ex
Boletus oratipes	e	Leotia lubrica	?
Boletus russellii	e	Leotia viscosa	?
Boletus subveutipes	XX	Lycoperdon perlatum (puff-ball)	ex
Cantharellus cibarius	ex	Lycoperdon pyriforme	e
Cantharellus ignicolor	e	Neolecta irregularis	x
Clavulina amethystina	e	Phellodon melaseucus	?
Clavulinopsis fusiformis	e	Polyporus brumalis	?
Cordyceps capitata	x	Ramaria formosa	XX
Craterellus cornucopioides	ex	Sarcodon imbricatus	e
Dacrymyces palmatus	EN	Suillus cavipes	e
Gomphus floccos	x	Suillus granulatus	e
Helvella lacunosa	EN	Suillus intermedius	e

Suillus luteus	e	**GILLED MUSHROOMS**	
Suillus pictus	e		
Tylopilus chromapes	e	Hygrophorus marginatus	e
Tylopilus eximius	EN	Hygrophorus nitidus	?
		Hygrophorus olivaceoalbus	e
		Hygrophorus parvulus	?
GILLED MUSHROOMS		Hygrophorus pratensis	ex
		Hygrophorus russula	e
Agaricus campestris	ex	Hygrophorus subviolaceus	?
Amanita citrina	x	Hygrophorus tennesseenisis	?
Amanita flavoconia	?	Hygrophorus tephroleucus	?
Amanita fulva	?	Hygrophorus unguinosus	?
Amanita rugescens		Hypholoma capnoides	?
(blusher)	e	Hypholoma sublateritium	e
Aminita virosa		Laccaria amethystea	e
(destroying angel)	XX	Laccaria laccata	e
Armillaria caligata	e	Laccaria ochropurpurea	e
Armillaria ponderosa	ex	Lactarius chrysorrheus	XX
Armillarlella mellea		Lactarius deceptivus	e
(honey mushroom)	ex	Lactarius deliciosus	ex
Cantharellula umbonata	e	Lactarius glyciosmus	e
Clitocybe clavipes	?	Lactarius lignyotus	EN
Collybia acervata	x	Lactarius mucidus	x
Collybia dryophila	x	Lactarius subparpureus	EN
Collybia maculata	x	Lactarius vellereus	x
Coprinus atramentarius	EN	Lactarius volemus	ex
Coprinus comatus	e	Marasimius oroades	e
Cortinarius armillatus	x	Marasimius rotula	?
Cortinarius evernius	x	Mycena galericulata	e
Cortinarius limonius	x	Mycena leaiana	?
Cortinarius semisanguineus	?	Panaeolus campanulatus	XX
Cystoderma amianthinum	?	Panellus serotinus	EN
Entoloma salmoneum	XX	Pholiota squarrosa	XX
Galerina autumnalis	XX	Psathyrella delineata	?
Gomphidius glutinosus	e	Russula brevipes	x
Hygrophoropsis aurantiaca	?	Russula densifolia	x
Hygrophorus cantharellus	?	Russula paludosa	e
Hygrophorus chlorophanus	?	Russula sanguinea	x
Hygrophorus chrysodon	e	Tricholoma flavovirens	e
Hygrophorus coccineus	e	Tricholoma portentosum	e
Hygrophorus eburneus	e	Tricholoma saponaceum	x
Hygrophorus fuligineus	?	Tricholomopsis platyphylla	e
Hygrophorus gliocyclus	?	Xerophalina campanella	x

GLOSSARY

barachois pond	A pond created by long shore currents. These oceanic currents cause spits to form on two sides. When these spits unite, fresh water is trapped behind, creating a barachois pond.
brackish	Fresh and saltwater mixed together.
clear-cut	When someone cuts down everything in the forest.
conglomerates	A type of sedimentary rock with different sizes of older rocks embedded in it.
dikes	Intrusions of molten igneous rocks into cracks in the existing bedrock.
extirpation	A term meaning locally extinct.
fjord	A deep bay created by glaciers.
gneiss	A type of rock which is often metamorphosed granite.
gypsum	A type of sedimentary rock created in shallow warm seas.
introduced species	Animals or plants that, through human activity, were brought to a place where they previously did not live.
mastodon	Pre-historic elephant-like creature. Evidenced in Cape Breton as 60,000 year old fossil.

petroglyph | Drawings on rocks by people of an earlier age.

red eft | The juvenile stage of red spotted newts, a type of salamander.

schist | A type of rock, often metamorphosed sedimentary rock.

sink hole | Formed when water dissolves an area of gypsum, causing the area to cave in.

talus slope | A hillside of loose rocks, caused by chemical weathering.

terrane | Referring to a specific and distinct section of the Earth's crust.

tombolo beach | Formed between an island and the main land by long shore currents.

0 Miles	60	Miles
0 Kilometres	100	Kilometres

1 Kilometre = (approx.) 6/10 Mile

SELECTED BIBLIOGRAPHY

Aucoin, Rene, Tim Reynolds and Betty Rooney (eds). 1982.
Hiking Trails of Cape Breton Highlands National Park.
Cheticamp, N.S.: Les Amis du Plein Air. 62 pp.

Barr, S.M., R.A. Jamieson and R.P. Raeside. The Cabot Trail
– A Journey Through Time. Draft No. 6, July 1992, 52 pp.

Belland. Personal Communication. Mosses of Victoria and
Inverness Counties, Cape Breton Island, Nova Scotia.

Bentley, P.A., Smith, E.C. 1956. The Forests of Cape Breton in the
17th and 18th Centuries, Nova Scotia Institute of Science.
Vol. XXIV part 1

Crum, Howard. 1976. Mosses of the Great Lakes Forest.
Ann Arbor: University of Michigan Herbarium. 404 pp.

Department of Natural Resources, Nova Scotia. The Margaree-
Lake Ainslie River System – Cape Breton Island,
Nova Scotia, 4 pp.

Department of Natural Resources. 1992. Provincial Hiking Trails
of Victoria County, Cape Breton Island. Baddeck, NS,
pamphlet.

Egginton, P.A. and J.T. Andrews. 1989. Sea Levels are Changing.
GEOS 89/2: 15–22.

Environment Canada, Parks Service. 1990. Walking in
the Highlands. A guide to the trails of Cape Breton
National Park. 16 pp.

Erskine, Anthony J. 1992. Atlas of Breeding Birds of the
Maritime Provinces. Halifax: Nova Scotia Museum, 270 pp.

Gilhen, John. 1984. Amphibians and Reptiles of Nova Scotia. Halifax: Nova Scotia Museum. 162 pp.

Godfrey, Earl W. 1958. Birds of Cape Breton Island, Nova Scotia, The Canadian Field Naturalist.

Hay, Keith. 1979. Guide to Identification of Whales in Newfoundland – Labrador Waters. Department of Fisheries and Oceans, St. John's, Newfoundland. 21 pp.

Hoyt, Erich. 1984. The Whales of Canada. Camden East, Ontario: Camden House Publishing. 127 pp.

Lafontaine, J.D., et. al. (eds). 1987. The Insects, Spiders and Mites of Cape Breton Highlands National Park. Biosystematics Research Centre, Agriculture Canada. 302 pp.

Lawley, David. 1984. Wildflower Blooming Sequence Western Side (Cheticamp). Cape Breton Highlands National Park. Pamphlet.

Les Amis du Plein Air. Birds of Cape Breton Highlands National Park

Raeside R.P. and S.M. Barr. 1992. Geology of the Northern and Eastern Cape Breton Highlands, Nova Scotia. Paper 89–14. Geological Survey of Canada, Ottawa. 39 pp.

Roland, A.E. 1982. Geological Background and Physiography of Nova Scotia. Halifax: Nova Scotia Institute of Science. 311 pp.

Roland, A.E. and E.C Smith. 1969. The Flora of Nova Scotia. Halifax: The Nova Scotia Museum. 746 pp.

Scott, Frederick. 1968. The Seals of Nova Scotian Waters. Halifax: Nova Scotia Museum. 9 pp.

Scott, Fred. 1993. Checklist of the Mammals of Nova Scotia. Official Nova Scotia Museum list.

Simmons, M., D. Davis, L. Griffiths and A. Muecke. 1984. Natural History of Nova Scotia, Nova Scotia Department of Education and Department of Lands and Forests, Halifax. 2 Vols, 807 pp.

Stewart, Colin. 1984 (5th ed). Hiking Trails of Nova Scotia. Canadian Hostelling Association, Nova Scotia. 96 pp.

Wallace, Elaine. 1985. Fact Sheet of Cape Breton Highlands National Park. Environment Canada. Pamphlet.

Watts, Jane. 1985. Mammals of Cape Breton Highlands National Park. Cheticamp, NS: Les Amis du Plein Air. 31 pp.

Whitehead, Ike. 1984 (4th ed). Hiking Trails of Nova Scotia. Canadian Hostelling Association, Nova Scotia.

Observations

Observations